SO-BQY-843

The
Constitutional
Convention

Other Books in the History Firsthand series:

The
Constitutional
Convention

Richard Haesly, *Book Editor*

Bonnie Szumski, *Editorial Director*
Scott Barbour, *Managing Editor*
David M. Haugen, *Series Editor*

Greenhaven Press, Inc., San Diego, California

Every effort has been made to trace the owners of copyrighted material. The articles in this volume may have been edited for content, length, and/or reading level. The titles have been changed to enhance the editorial purpose.

Library of Congress Cataloging-in-Publication Data

The Constitutional Convention / Richard Haesly, book editor.
        p. cm.—(History firsthand)
    Includes bibliographical references and index.
    ISBN 0-7377-1071-3 (pbk. : alk. paper)—ISBN 0-7377-1072-1
(lib. : alk. paper)
    1. Constitutional history—United States—Sources. 2. Constitutional conventions—United States—History—Sources. I. Haesly, Richard, 1969– II. Series.

KF4510.C657 2002
342.73'024--dc21   2001023832

Contents

Chapter 1: Signs of a Failing System

Chapter Preface   41

1. An Early Critique of the Articles of Confederation
by Alexander Hamilton   43
Alexander Hamilton, a strong believer in a power-
ful national government, writes to his friend John
Duane, a New York delegate to the Confederation
Congress. In his letter, Hamilton complains that the
Articles of Confederation are fundamentally flawed
because they do not give Congress any real authority.

2. Caution Against a Constitutional Convention
*by the Massachusetts Delegation to the Confed-
eration Congress*   52
In 1785 states began petitioning the Confederation
Congress to call a convention in order to address
problems with the Articles of Confederation. On
September 3, 1785, the Massachusetts delegation to
the Confederation Congress cautioned its governor
and legislature that such a convention might not be
an advisable or legal remedy to their concerns.

3. General Washington Worries About Shays's Rebellion
by George Washington   58
General George Washington, although officially
retired, maintained an interest in American politics, especially when something as destabilizing as
Shays's Rebellion occurred. In two letters, Washington expresses his concern over the possible disastrous results of the rebellion for a nation he was
so instrumental in creating.

4. A Prominent Woman Analyzes Shays's Rebellion
by Abigail Adams   63
Abigail Adams provides Thomas Jefferson, who
was in Paris as the U.S. ambassador to France,

with details about the causes of and early skirmishes in Shays's Rebellion. Being a prominent Boston woman, she is privy to the latest news about the rebellion; however, her high social status may color her assessment of the rebels' motives.

Chapter 2: The Workings of the Convention

could about the early workings of the convention. The secrecy under which the convention operated limits what Carrington can write, but he is able to present a picture of how fundamental the changes to the Articles of Confederation will be if the convention delegates get their way.

Chapter 3: Major Debates in the Convention

preferred by the large states) or equal representation for each state (as the small states wanted).

Chapter 4: Reactions to the Finished Product

December 20, 1787, letter to his friend, James
Madison, an important contributor to the
Constitution.

Chapter 5: The Ratification Debate and the Bill of Rights

Alexander Hamilton, a strong proponent of the
U.S. Constitution, attempts to persuade his fellow

and closely divided New York delegates to agree to ratify the document. He explains that the present system of government is fundamentally flawed, that mere modification of the Articles of Confederation is neither possible nor desirable, and that the U.S. Constitution "will answer . . . all the beneficial purposes of society."

Foreword

In his preface to a book on the events leading to the Civil War, Stephen B. Oates, the historian and biographer of Abraham Lincoln, John Brown, and other noteworthy American historical figures, explained the difficulty of writing history in the traditional third-person voice of the biographer and historian. "The trouble, I realized, was the detached third-person voice," wrote Oates. "It seemed to wring all the life out of my characters and the antebellum era." Indeed, how can a historian, even one as prominent as Oates, compete with the eloquent voices of Daniel Webster, Abraham Lincoln, Harriet Beecher Stowe, Frederick Douglass, and Robert E. Lee?

Oates's comment notwithstanding, every student of history, professional and amateur alike, can name a score of excellent accounts written in the traditional third-person voice of the historian that bring to life an event or an era and the people who lived through it. In *Battle Cry of Freedom*, James M. McPherson vividly re-creates the American Civil War. Barbara Tuchman's *The Guns of August* captures in sharp detail the tensions in Europe that led to the outbreak of World War I. Taylor Branch's *Parting the Waters* provides a detailed and dramatic account of the American Civil Rights Movement. The study of history would be impossible without such guiding texts.

Nonetheless, Oates's comment makes a compelling point. Often the most convincing tellers of history are those who lived through the event, the eyewitnesses who recorded their firsthand experiences in autobiographies, speeches, memoirs, journals, and letters. The Greenhaven Press History Firsthand series presents history through the words of first-person narrators. Each text in this series captures a significant historical era or event—the American Civil War, the

Great Depression, the Holocaust, the Roaring 20s, the 1960s, the Vietnam War. Readers will investigate these historical eras and events by examining primary-source documents, authored by chroniclers both famous and little known. The texts in the History Firsthand series comprise the celebrated and familiar words of the presidents, generals, and famous men and women of letters who recorded their impressions for posterity, as well as the statements of the ordinary people who struggled to understand the storm of events around them—the foot soldiers who fought the great battles and their loved ones back home, the men and women who waited on the breadlines, the college students who marched in protest.

The texts in this series are particularly suited to students beginning serious historical study. By examining these firsthand documents, novice historians can begin to form their own insights and conclusions about the historical era or event under investigation. To aid the student in that process, the texts in the History Firsthand series include introductions that provide an overview of the era or event, timelines, and annotated bibliographies that point the serious student toward key historical works for further study.

The study of history commences with an examination of words—the testimony of witnesses who lived through an era or event and left for future generations the task of making sense of their accounts. The Greenhaven Press History Firsthand series invites the beginner historian to commence the process of historical investigation by focusing on the words of those individuals who made history by living through it and recording their experiences firsthand.

Introduction

The story of the U.S. Constitution does not begin with the signing of the document on September 17, 1787, nor with the ninth state ratifying it and thereby establishing it as the supreme law of the land. Nor does the story begin with the Philadelphia convention attended by some of the most prominent Americans of their day in the hot, sweltering summer of 1787. In fact, the story of the U.S. Constitution begins over a decade earlier. It starts with the American colonies' announcement that they considered themselves free of British rule and their subsequent effort to establish a new government.

On July 4, 1776, the American colonies announced their plan to break all ties with Britain. This announcement took the form of one of the most famous documents of human history, the Declaration of Independence. However, the Declaration of Independence, no matter how revolutionary it was, no matter how important it remains to America's founding principles, was not a legal document, nor did it create a government. It simply declared that the American colonies were free from the rule of Britain. Until a formal government could be formed, the colonies were ruled by their individual state governments and by a temporary national legislature, the Continental Congress.

On November 15, 1777, however, the Continental Congress voted to accept a plan of government called the Articles of Confederation and Perpetual Union. More succinctly, this plan of government is referred to as the Articles of Confederation. At the heart of this document was the principle that "each state should retain its sovereignty, freedom and independence and every power, jurisdiction and right not expressly delegated to the Union government." In other words, the national government, under the Articles of Confederation, was extremely limited in its powers. The national government could only do what the individual states would allow it to do. Finally, after four years of debate, all thirteen American states ratified the plan. In 1781 the new nation had its first system of government, the Articles of Confederation.

An Overview of the Articles' Powers and Procedures

A weak national government was precisely what the thirteen states wanted. One of the main reasons that they decided to declare their independence from Britain was to escape rule by a British Parliament in which they had no representation. The states did not want to make the same mistake by creating an American national legislature that they could not control. Each state wanted to protect its own interests in the new government. Secondly, although the Articles of Confederation referred to a "perpetual union," the thirteen states were very different from one another. Massachusetts and New York, with an emphasis on finance and trade, were very different from the agricultural economies of North Carolina and Georgia. The Northern and Southern states also disagreed over the morality and utility of slavery. Pierce Butler, a South Carolina delegate to the Constitutional Convention, wrote that the interests of the North and the South were "as different as the interests of Russia and Turkey."[1] The states wanted to ensure that under the new system of government their economies and way of life would not be threatened by a strong central government that would most likely bend to the will of the most prosperous or populous states.

Under the Articles of Confederation each state retained the power to name its own delegates to the national congress and to pay them. Each state had one vote in the legislature, regardless of its population or economic power. Each state could recall its delegates and substitute others whenever they wanted. This power of the states to "hire" and "fire" their representatives at will ensured that the national congress was made up of boosters for the individual states—representatives who had little interest in sacrificing state policies for a national agenda.

Although the Articles of Confederation gave the national government the authority to negotiate treaties and to provide a national defense, it relied on the individual state governments to collect the taxes that would be necessary to pay for these activities. If a state did not want to pay its share, as many states did not, then Congress had no power to compel those states to contribute more. For example, America had accumulated $42 million in war debts while fighting the British in the War of Independence. The states only paid a fraction of this amount. Congress asked the states to contribute $12 million; it received around $3 million. Some states, such as North Carolina and Georgia, refused to pay anything. Money was such a problem for the national government under the Articles of Confederation that when Algerian pirates held American sailors hostage in 1785, the national government could only offer $200 per captured sailor. The pirates demanded more money, and while the government gathered together the necessary ransom, several hostages died of the plague.

The states were more concerned with building their own economies than with the financial well-being of the country as a whole. National agreements with foreign countries, for example, did not preclude individual states from laying their own import or export taxes as they saw fit. Therefore, when John Adams negotiated a trade agreement with Great Britain he was famously asked, "Would you like one treaty or thirteen, Mr. Adams?"[2]

The lack of a united effort was apparent in more than just economic matters. Under the Articles of Confederation, no independent executive existed. In other words, there was no president who could speak for the country or who could act quickly and decisively when the situation warranted a rapid response. All decisions were made by committees of the Congress, by the full Congress, or by the thirteen separate states. All of this made it extremely difficult for any work to get done. All decisions made by the Congress had to be approved by a supramajority of at least nine states. Furthermore, any amendments to the Articles of Confederation required unanimous consent by all thirteen states. Given that the thirteen states rarely agreed on anything, these voting rules virtually instituted gridlock in the Congress. According to historians Broadus Mitchell and Louise Pearson Mitchell, "Congress was inhibited and frustrated. The members, collectively, would have been fit patients for the psychiatrist. They were yanked in fourteen different directions, by commands and suspicions of their states, and by their obligations to the general government."[3]

Ironically, these weaknesses in the fundamental procedures of the Articles of Confederation may have actually hastened the creation of a much stronger national government under the U.S. Constitution. By seeing how flawed the system of government was under the Articles of Confederation, prominent politicians were slowly forced to accept that an entirely new system of government might be needed. As scholar Jack N. Rokove concludes,

> The Constitutional Convention was made possible only by the collapse of all previous attempts to amend the Articles of Confederation. . . . Only after the futility of [these amendment procedures] became evident could would-be reformers of the Confederation begin to think seriously about what the establishment of a national government would entail.[4]

The Successes and Failures of the Articles of Confederation

Despite the fundamental weaknesses of the system of government under the Articles of Confederation, they were not a complete failure. As the noted constitutional historian Clinton Rossiter argues, "The record of the Confederation government was not wholly bad, and the years between 1774 and 1789 should be judged as a period of useful (if also nearly fatal) experiment rather than of inglorious folly."[5] What were the principal successes? First, the Articles of Confederation (in addition to the Continental Congress, which preceded it) oversaw the American Revolutionary army that had defeated Great Britain, one of the world's most powerful countries in the late eighteenth century. Second, the Articles of Confederation saw its diplomatic corps forge important alliances and gain financial assistance from European powers, such as France and Spain. This diplomatic corps was also responsible for the Treaty of Paris of 1783, which legally established American independence from Great Britain. Third, although it was weak, the National Congress of the Articles of Confederation did provide important political experience to young politicians who would play a critical role in the Constitutional Convention— such as James Madison, Alexander Hamilton, and Charles Pinckney. More importantly, the experience that these men gained was at the national, rather than simply at the state, level. Fourth, the Articles of Confederation oversaw some early sacrifices made in the name of national unity. For example, Virginia and New York both relinquished claims on lands to their west in order to convince Maryland to ratify the Articles of Confederation. Finally, the inability of the Articles of Confederation to deal with certain national crises served as an obvious bad example for those who attempted to forge a new system of government in the Constitutional Convention of 1787.

Despite the successes, as time went on, it became increasingly clear that the Articles of Confederation were seriously flawed. Some observers saw these problems earlier than others. Even before the Articles of Confederation were ratified by all thirteen states, critics, such as Alexander Hamilton (George Washington's aide-de-camp during the Revolutionary War), were expressing concern that the national government under the Articles of Confederation was too weak. For example, the national government was ineffective in solving important problems such as land disputes between states. Land disputes arose because some states, when they were originally chartered as colonies, were given rights to all of the land to their west while other states had more limited charters. Additionally, the charters were often vague (since those writing the charters did not know the geography of the land that they were chartering), which led to competing claims over the same land. Land was important because, as historian

Richard Bernstein argues, it was "the most durable and reliable measure of wealth and power in eighteenth century America. . . . A state's territory was a potentially valuable source of revenue that could keep taxes down and, after sale to farmers and settlers, contribute still further to the state's economic growth."[6] Therefore, a system of government that

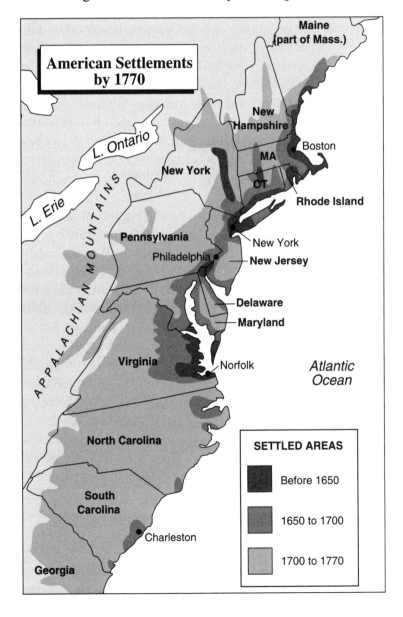

American Settlements
by 1770

Maine
(part of Mass.)

New
Hampshire

L. Ontario

Boston

MA

New York

CT

L. Erie

Rhode Island

APPALACHIAN MOUNTAINS

Pennsylvania

New York

Philadelphia

New Jersey

Delaware

Maryland

Virginia

Norfolk

Atlantic
Ocean

North Carolina

SETTLED AREAS

Before 1650

South
Carolina

1650 to 1700

Charleston

1700 to 1770

Georgia

allowed a small number of states to block any action by the national government would be one that would make land disputes difficult to address. At times, these land disputes even led to violence, as was the case of the 1781 "border wars" surrounding Vermont's desire to become independent from New York and New Hampshire. Also, Vermont's attempt to claim independence included a deal whereby it would agree to become a British colony again if Britain would support it in its bid to separate from New York. Therefore, this land dispute threatened not simply New York and New Hampshire but also the integrity of the new American nation. Congress, therefore, offered Vermont statehood. However, after Vermont broke off negotiations with Britain, Congress reneged on its deal because New York, New Hampshire, and Massachusetts opposed the idea and several other states wanted Congress to deal with other matters. It was not until 1791 that Vermont became the first new state to enter the Union.

Perhaps the greatest problem of the government under the Articles of Confederation was its inability to regulate commerce among the states. The Revolutionary War obviously cut off one of America's strongest trading partners, Britain. To offset this loss, the states needed to increase trade with each other. Unfortunately, the states tended to view other states as competitors rather than as trading partners. States were primarily interested in protecting the industries located in their states, so they would place high tariffs on goods coming from other states, even if those states could sell their goods more cheaply than the local industries being protected by the high tariffs. Furthermore, states such as New York, Massachusetts, and Virginia were unwilling to share the economic benefits that they reaped from their thriving ports. The taxes that these states levied on goods coming in or going out were important sources of revenue for these states, but the taxes also caused resentment from the states that had to rely on these ports to ship their goods abroad. For example, Virginia passed a law that any ship failing to pay duty in one of its ports could be seized by any Virginia citizen, with one half of the proceeds going to the informer and one half to the state government. This law was not intended for ships from Spain or France; it was primarily aimed at cargo from Pennsylvania, Maryland, and Massachusetts.

The Annapolis Convention

To address this matter, in September 1786 delegates from five states met in Annapolis, Maryland, to discuss ways to improve interstate trade among the American states. The Annapolis Convention grew out of a compact between Virginia and Maryland, which had successfully resolved long-standing arguments over navigation rights on the Potomac and Chesapeake Rivers. Based on their experience negotiating agreements with Maryland, Virginia had asked Congress to call for the Annapolis Convention "to consider how far a universal system in their commercial relations may be necessary to their common interest and their permanent harmony."

Although all thirteen states had been invited to attend the convention, only five states (Delaware, New Jersey, Virginia, New York, and Pennsylvania) participated—and only the first three of these had full delegations. In fact, even Maryland failed to send delegates to this convention, which was held in its own state. The New Jersey legislature had sent its delegation with instructions to consider ways to strengthen the national government in more than simply commercial issues. Alexander Hamilton, one of the New York delegates, had wanted to increase Congress's power since 1780, and he took advantage of the New Jersey delegation's broad instructions and the small number of delegates to encourage the adoption of a strong resolution.

The end result of the Annapolis Convention was a resolution that called for a convention in Philadelphia to start in May 1787 to "devise further provisions as shall appear to them necessary to render the constitution of the Federal Government adequate to the exigencies of the Union." This resolution was submitted to the Confederation Congress, which delayed action and watered down the wording but, in the end, agreed to the principle of a convention to be held starting in May 1787.

Therefore, although the Annapolis Convention was in many ways a resounding failure, it also provided the important spark that eventually led to the radical step of replacing the Articles of Confederation with an entirely new system of government. Even though not everyone was convinced that it was necessary, a larger number of prominent politicians from several states began to think about how a new government might look. Historian Rokove describes the true contribution of the Annapolis Convention to the history of the American Constitution in the following way:

> During the months that followed the adjournment of the Annapolis Convention in September 1786 . . . it at last became possible to fashion a new agenda of reform far more expansive than anything that had been considered previously. Instead of vesting modest additional powers in the existing Congress, reformers . . . could now seriously envision a radical transfer of authority from the states to a national government that would be reconstructed along more familiar lines, with an independent executive and judiciary enforcing the laws formed by a bicameral legislature.[7]

Shays's Rebellion

Therefore, the Annapolis Convention suggested that some states were beginning to consider the possibility of amending the Articles of Confederation in order to strengthen some of the document's obvious weaknesses. However, the reasons for the articles' weaknesses (especially the fact that each state was jealous of its own power and refused to make concessions to facilitate the functioning of the national government) also explained why a solution was so difficult to achieve. All of this changed, however, with Shays's Rebellion of 1786.

Shays's Rebellion grew out of a problem that was common throughout the states in the 1780s. The states owed a considerable amount of money for the debts that accrued during the Revolutionary War. Although some of this debt was owed to wealthy Americans, much was owed to foreigners and foreign governments. If the states wanted to begin paying on these foreign debts, which they needed to do if they were to establish trading ties to replace their reliance on British trade, they had to raise taxes. These increased taxes placed a heavy burden on the farmers, many of whom had let their fields lay fallow in order to fight in the Revolutionary War. Each state needed their farmers to pay their debts so that the state could pay off its debts. Those who could not pay would have their farms foreclosed and were forced to auction off their possessions to raise the necessary money.

From 1784 to 1786 in Hampshire County, Massachusetts, nearly one-third of the males over the age of sixteen were involved in debt cases. Within that time, seventy-three men in Hampshire County alone were thrown into debtors' prison for failing to pay their taxes. Farmers would look to their state legislature for assistance. They might ask their legislatures for stay laws, which would delay debt payments for a year; tender laws, which would require creditors to accept depreciated money (rather than the gold or silver that many demanded); or simply printing of more money.

Creditors obviously rejected all of these solutions out of hand. From 1784 to 1787 New Jersey, South Carolina, Pennsylvania, Virginia, Maryland, and Massachusetts all had some instances of farmers protesting the foreclosure of their lands and property, usually by forcibly closing the auctions or the circuit courts. In some cases, courthouses were burned in hopes of destroying the court records and thus ending any legal proceedings against the indebted individuals.

Most states were able to impose order. Massachusetts was different. Bankers and merchants dominated the Massachusetts legislature to such a degree that many rural communities in western Massachusetts did not even bother to send their elected representatives because it would be a waste of time and money (since their views would automatically be voted down). Thus, the Massachusetts farmers were trapped by large—and growing—personal debts as well as by a legislature that ignored their concerns. Out of frustration, they took matters into their own hands. Daniel Shays, a farmer and Revolutionary War hero, became their leader. Bands of farmers under Shays's direction would forcibly stop auctions and would not allow circuit courts to sit. They also began intimidating and robbing wealthy industrialists and bankers.

The Massachusetts government wanted the national government to send the national army to put down the rebellion. Congress consented and asked the states to contribute $530,000 to the cause. All states, except Virginia, refused to pay their share, mostly because they did not want to spend their money on what they believed to be a "Massachusetts problem." Massachusetts eventually called together its own state militia, headed by General Benjamin Lincoln, which successfully put down the rebellion in January and February 1787.

Shays's Rebellion was never successful enough to threaten the authority or the legitimacy of the Massachusetts government. However, the implications of the uprising made it much more than simply a "Massachusetts problem." Prominent citizens and politicians from across the country feared that their states might soon face a rebellion similar to the one that Massachusetts experienced. Massachusetts was widely believed to have one of the best state constitutions. Therefore, if Massachusetts could not avoid such internal turmoil and if no state could rely on the national congress to provide any assistance, the independence that America had fought so hard to achieve could be threatened from within. As historians Christopher Collier and James Lincoln Collier suggest,

> If many ordinary people were upset by Shays' Rebellion, however, the people of wealth, who supplied much of the leadership of the country were simply horrified by it. In particular it seemed bizarre that the national government had stood helplessly by, lacking the legal authority to put the rebellion down. To men like [James] Madison and [George] Washington, Shays' Rebellion was an imperative. It hung like a shadow over the old Congress, and gave both impetus and urgency to the Constitutional Convention. It was the final, irrefutable piece of evidence that something had gone badly wrong. For some time, these men had known that the deficiencies of the American government must be remedied. Shays' Rebellion made it clear to them that it must be done *now*.[8]

The Constitutional Convention

Those leaders who began to believe that the Articles of Confederation were inadequate to address the problems facing the new nation had the perfect forum in which to express their concerns. The Annapolis Convention had called for another convention to be held starting on the second Monday in May 1787. The upheaval of Shays's Rebellion ensured that the Confederation Congress would echo this call for a convention. On February 21, 1787, the Congress officially announced what it hoped would be a meeting to discuss minor changes to the Articles of Confederation. In fact, this meeting would turn out to be the Constitutional Convention. Instead of minor changes to the Articles of Confederation, a whole new governing structure would be born.

The convention was scheduled to begin work in Philadelphia on the second Monday in May (May 14, 1787). However, it could not officially begin work until May 25, when a quorum of delegates from seven states had arrived in Philadelphia. Philadelphia proudly hosted the convention. The city showed its pleasure in several ways. Many of its prominent citizens threw parties for the delegates as they arrived. The newspapers announced the convention and wrote with glowing praise about the convention and its delegates. The city also placed gravel outside of the State House, where the convention was held, to keep passing horses and carriages quiet for the framers as they worked at building a new government.

The Delegates to the Convention

Twelve of the thirteen states sent delegates to the Constitutional Convention. Rhode Island, which had consistently disagreed with the other states throughout much of the 1780s, chose not to participate. In fact, one Boston newspaper referred to Rhode Island as "Rogue Island" and suggested that it "be dropped out of the Union or apportioned to the different States which surround her."[9]

The state legislatures selected many of their most distinguished citizens to be delegates to the Constitutional Convention. In all, seventy-four delegates were named by twelve state legislatures to attend the convention. Fifty-five delegates actually attended the convention, although many of them arrived late or left early. The other nineteen delegates who were appointed but did not attend were either unable or unwilling due to various personal or business reasons.

Some of those who attended had international reputations, such as George Washington, the leader of the American army during the Revolutionary War, and Benjamin Franklin, a world-renowned essayist, inventor, and statesman, who had served for many years as an ambassador to France. Others, such as Alexander Hamilton and James Madison, were not known outside of the United States but had begun to build strong national reputations because of their roles in the Confederation Congress and in national forums, such as the Annapolis Convention. One of the delegates, Roger Sherman of Connecticut, not only signed the Declaration of Independence but also served on the committee that wrote it. Also attending the conference were prominent state-level politicians, such as Edmund Randolph, the governor of Virginia; Luther Martin, the attorney general of Maryland for over three decades; and William Paterson, the attorney general for New Jersey.

Although not entirely representative of the country's diverse population (since most of the delegates were wealthy men), the delegates came from a fair number of professions. Many of the delegates had more than one profession. In all, there were thirty-four lawyers, twenty-seven farmers, thirty creditors, ten public servants, and seven merchants. Many of the delegates had demonstrated their public spirit in the past. Eight of the delegates had been signers of the Declaration of Independence, and thirty had served in the army during the Revolutionary War. Many of these delegates went on to play prominent roles (as presidents, vice presidents, Supreme Court justices, members of Congress, and cabinet secretaries) in the new federal government.

Despite the strong credentials of those who attended the convention, some rather eminent individuals did not or could not attend. For example, two later presidents, John Adams and Thomas Jefferson, were both abroad, serving as American ambassadors in Europe. The passionate Virginian Patrick

Henry, who had once famously said in defense of his position to support American independence from Britain, "Give me liberty or give me death!" was selected as a Virginia delegate, but he declined the appointment because he said that he "smelled a rat." He sensed that the convention would be doing much more than simply modifying the Articles of Confederation, and he believed that such changes would threaten individual rights. Thomas Paine, another important figure in the months leading up to the Revolutionary War—his pamphlet *Common Sense* was a rousing justification for independence from Britain—was off in Europe trying to get investors to allow him to build some iron bridges that he had recently designed. Samuel Adams, a noted Boston firebrand, often a thorn in the side of the British as the leader of the group responsible for the Boston Tea Party, was not selected by the Massachusetts legislature to be one of its four delegates. John Adams welcomed the absence of many of these revolutionaries because he believed that some people are better at tearing down a government than they are at trying to build one. Even without these figures, when Thomas Jefferson received word in Paris (where he was serving as the American ambassador to France) about who would be attending the convention, he wrote to John Adams and described the convention delegates as a group of demigods.

Why did these prominent individuals agree to spend such a long time away from their businesses and their families? Why did some delegates travel great distances in order to participate? (The Georgia delegates had to travel over eight hundred miles on horse.) Why did others attend even though it meant great personal hardship? (George Washington almost did not attend because his brother had died and because his rheumatism was so bad that he could not even lift his arms to his head only a few months before the convention began.) The reasons why these men put aside their own hardships are varied. Shays's Rebellion and other crises had convinced many of them that their young country was in serious danger of disintegrating if new rules of government were not drafted. At the same time, they also wanted to make sure that whatever changes were made would not harm their states' interests. In addition, forging a new government was an intellectual challenge that many of the framers simply could not pass up. Finally, the Constitutional Convention, if successful, could help the framers to achieve fame—both in their immediate political careers and perhaps for posterity.

The Process of Creating a New Government

Once enough delegates had arrived, the convention could begin its work. On May 25, 1787, the first day of the convention, George Washington was unanimously elected as the president of the convention. Benjamin Franklin, as the convention's oldest and most respected member as well as a delegate from the host state of Pennsylvania, was scheduled to make the speech nominating Washington. However, the rainy weather on the first day of the convention aggravated Franklin's gout, so another Pennsylvania delegate, Robert Morris, read Franklin's speech.

At this first session, the convention also appointed a committee to determine the rules for the debates. The committee proposed and the convention accepted these rules. All decisions in the convention were made by a simple majority vote, with each state getting one vote. To avoid rash decisions, they adopted an ancient debating device, created by the English Parliament, the Committee of the Whole. When the convention was in the Committee of the Whole, no decision was ever final. They could go back to modify any decision, even if a majority had already voted in favor of a given provision. This allowed them to rethink earlier decisions in light of later choices, thereby decreasing the chances of internal contradictions in the final document.

The delegates needed this flexibility to return to decisions that they had made previously because they faced a series of fundamental questions that had to be addressed. First, based on their frustrations during Shays's Rebellion, many of the delegates wanted to know how to enable the national government with both the power to declare war and the means to wage it while at the same time ensuring that the government would never turn on its own citizens. Second, they wondered if representation could occur on the national level, or if it would be the case that those in the national legislature would ignore the wishes of those who elected them. Third, recognizing the various regional issues that divided them, how could each state protect its local and regional interests, especially if it might end up holding the perpetual minority position? Finally, could these problems be solved by fixing the Articles of Confederation, or should the delegates build a new government from scratch?

The basic question of whether to amend the Articles of Confederation or to scrap them entirely and start over from the beginning was answered almost immediately. On May 29, the first day that the convention began to debate substantive issues, Washington recognized his fellow Virginia delegate Edmund Randolph. Randolph, with the assistance of another Virginia delegate, James Madison, described an entirely new system of government, with a considerably stronger national government than the one under the Articles of Confederation. Randolph, the young governor of Virginia, presented the plan to the convention, although most of it was designed by Madison, because Randolph was considered to be a more charismatic speaker. Their plan, called the Virginia Plan, became the basis of debate for the first two weeks of the convention. Although delegates disagreed with specific aspects of this plan, consideration of this proposal suggested that many delegates were inclined to start over rather than simply make small adjustments to the Articles of Confederation.

Obviously, by opting to design a new system of government, the delegates debated a wide range of ideas throughout the four-month convention. However, three issues stand out as the most important and the most contentious: representation, slavery, and the creation of a national executive, or president. First, the delegates needed to determine how states would be represented in the national legislature. Should all states have equal representation regardless of population—as they had in the Articles of Confederation— or should larger states have more seats in the legislature?

Related to the issue of representation was slavery, the second important debate during the convention. Slavery was related to apportioning the seats in the national legislature because the delegates needed to determine if slaves would be included in a state's population. This decision would also affect how much money each state would be expected to contribute to the national government since that, too, would be determined by population. Slavery itself was a contentious issue—so contentious that many of the delegates would have preferred to ignore it entirely. However, the role that slavery played in apportioning the national legislature forced this issue into the delegates' debates. Finally, the delegates needed to determine whether the new system of government would be headed by a president. Many felt that the lack of an individual leader of the country, who could act decisively in moments of crisis (such as during Shays's Rebellion), was a fundamental flaw in the Articles of Confederation. Others believed that the president would inevitably become an American king, a tyrant in the making.

Representation: The Virginia Plan, the New Jersey Plan, and the Great Compromise

Representation was the first of the three major debates that the convention confronted. Representation became the convention's first issue because the Virginia Plan proposed a bicameral legislature, with both houses to be apportioned by population. Virginia and the other large states argued that this made sense since they would be paying a larger share of the taxes that would be needed to make this new government run. They also approved because, as the more populous states, they would have more representatives in Congress and would be able to have greater influence over the laws that the national Congress would pass.

The small states worried that the larger states would be able to ignore the wishes of the small states if the Virginia Plan were adopted. William Paterson, a delegate from the small state of New Jersey, proposed a different system than the Virginia Plan. In the New Jersey Plan, there would be a single-chamber legislature, and each state would have equal representation in this chamber. Not surprisingly, the New Jersey Plan was voted down by the large states. However, the small states had made their voices heard, and they banded together to argue against adopting the Virginia Plan.

With the large states favoring the Virginia Plan and the small states favoring the New Jersey Plan, the convention faced a serious obstacle to designing a new system of government. For over a month, this issue divided and bedeviled the delegates. Eventually Roger Sherman, a delegate from Connecticut, proposed that there be a two-chamber legislature with one house based on population (the House of Representatives) and the other based on equal representation for all states regardless of population (the Senate). The convention, after much acrimonious debate, eventually accepted this plan, which has come to be known as the Great Compromise (or, in honor of the state Sherman represented, the Connecticut Compromise).

Calling this plan the Great Compromise is no exaggeration. Delegates on each side of the debate were passionate about their positions. James Madison, the primary architect of the Virginia Plan, methodically criticized and rejected every aspect of the New Jersey Plan. The small states were equally vehement in their opposition to the Virginia Plan, especially its (as the small states perceived it) built-in preference for protecting the interests of the larger states. Gunning Bedford, a Delaware delegate, went so far as to insinuate that, without equal representation in the legislature, the small states might leave the convention and "find some foreign ally of more honor and good faith who will take them by the hand and do them justice."[10] In other words, without the Great Compromise, not only would the convention have ended in failure, but it might have eventually led to the dissolution of the United States as well.

Slavery and the Three-Fifths Compromise

The second major debate in the Constitutional Convention also ended with a historic compromise. Although the word *slave* does not actively appear anywhere in the U.S. Constitution, slavery played a critical role during the Constitutional Convention. This is not surprising since slavery played an important role in the late-eighteenth-century American economy and society. According to the first census in 1790, almost one-fifth of the American population lived in slavery. Furthermore, the delegates from the South made it clear that any attempt to ban slavery would result in the Southern states leaving the convention. In general, therefore, although many delegates personally abhorred slavery, the convention did its best to avoid slavery in its deliberations.

Unfortunately, slavery was not simply a moral issue that could be put to one side. It affected a number of proposals in the system of government that the delegates were attempting to forge. Most importantly, slavery influenced the question of representation in the House of Representatives. The Southern states wanted slaves to be counted as part of their population when considering how many seats they would get in the House of Representatives. The Northern states, many of whom had already banned slavery in their states, worried that the Southern states could simply import more slaves to increase their representation in the House. The Southern states also believed, however, that slaves should not be counted as people in terms of calculating the amount of taxes that they would contribute to the new national government. The Northern states argued that if slaves could be used to increase the Southern states' representation in the House of Representatives, then they should be included in terms of calculating tax contributions.

In the end, the delegates of the Constitutional Convention compromised on this political and moral issue. Many of the delegates officially condemned slavery in their comments in the convention, but they agreed that the Constitution would not ban slavery. Additionally they adopted a provision from the 1783 Confederation Congress. In the infamous Three-Fifths Compromise, slaves would count as three-fifths of a person for population and tax purposes only. It did not grant slaves (where slavery was still legal) three-fifths of the rights granted to a free person. The three-fifths was only used as an accounting tool for apportioning seats in the House of Representatives and allocating taxes from and financial payments to the states.

The Presidency

The third fundamental debate in the convention concerned the creation of an executive branch of government. James Wilson, a Pennsylvania delegate, proposed to establish one national executive; in other words, he was suggesting that the new government have a president. Many delegates feared that such a system would inevitably devolve into a monarchy. The president, once in power, could use his powers to maintain his position and amass greater authority for himself at the expense of the other branches of government and the states. Despite these concerns, however, on June 4, by a vote of seven to three, the convention accepted Wilson's proposal, thereby creating the position of the American president.

How the president was to be selected also caused great consternation at the convention. In the end, a compromise would have to be reached in this area as well. Throughout the convention, the delegates returned to this issue time and again. The delegates variously proposed and debated a president elected by the Congress, one elected by the state legislatures, and one chosen by a body of electors selected by the states. Only a few of the delegates even mentioned the possibility of a direct election of the president by the voters. When the convention reached a topic that it could not resolve, it would often send it to the Committee on Postponed Matters for further consideration. The issue of how to elect the president was sent to this committee. It proposed the indirect election of the president to a term of four years, with no limitation on the number of terms that the president could serve. The indirect election would be made by an electoral college. Each state would receive a number of electors equal to the number of its representatives and senators in Congress. The convention adopted the committee's proposals, not because it thought it was perfect, but because it was the least objectionable of the various suggestions that had been made.

Signing the Document

Once the important compromises had been made and all of the details had been worked out, the convention appointed the Committee on Style and Arrangement to combine all of the ideas into a single document. On September 17, 1787, forty-two of the fifty-five delegates met together one last time. They gathered to consider the fruits of their labor. They assembled to sign the U.S. Constitution.

Benjamin Franklin, the oldest delegate and one of the most famous Americans of his time, urged all delegates in attendance to sign the document. Because it was the product of so many compromises, he admitted that the Constitution was not a perfect document. However, he firmly believed that it was the best that the convention could achieve given the diverse and passionate views expressed by the delegates. He also encouraged his fellow delegates to follow his lead in keeping their concerns to themselves. He noted that many of the delegates, including himself, had grave misgivings about various aspects of the final document. The debates were often acrimonious, but he pledged not to divulge to the public what had been said in the debates for fear that it would cause people to question the resolve of the convention delegates.

Despite stirring words from this venerable American statesman, three of the delegates in attendance on the last day of the convention refused to sign the U.S. Constitution. Two of those who refused to sign, George Mason and Elbridge Gerry, did not wish to add their names to the document because they wanted the Constitution to include a Bill of Rights, which would protect important citizen rights, such as freedom of speech and freedom of the press. The third delegate who refused to sign was Edmund Randolph. He refused to sign the Constitution not only because he had personal misgivings about the system of government that they had created, but he was also certain that the states would refuse to ratify the Constitution. Randolph wanted to be available to attend whatever subsequent convention would be called in the event that the Constitution was rejected by the states. If he signed the document, he thought that he might not be chosen as a delegate to this later convention.

Alexander Hamilton and many other convention delegates worried that, if the Constitution was not signed by all of the delegates present that day, opponents to the Constitution could use this fact as a weapon in the various state ratification conventions. Therefore, the convention decided to include a resolution that announced that, even if some individual delegates refused, all twelve states had unanimously agreed to sign the Constitution. In the end, thirty-nine of the forty-two delegates in attendance that final day of the convention signed the U.S. Constitution.

Ratification Debate and the Bill of Rights

Just as the story of the U.S. Constitution does not begin with its signing by thirty-nine delegates on September 17, 1787, nor does it end at that point either. In order to have the force of law, the new system of government described in the Constitution had to be approved by the Confederation Congress, which was still the legal authority in the United States, and ratified by at least nine of the thirteen states.

The Confederation Congress obliged quickly. On September 20, 1787, it received the Constitution. On September 28, 1787, after only one week of debate, Congress submitted the Constitution to the states for their consideration.

Some states responded immediately. The first state to ratify the Constitution, Delaware, did so unanimously on December 7, 1787. Pennsylvania, not unanimously but by a healthy two to one margin, and New Jersey, unanimously, followed suit on December 12 and December 18. Other states took much longer to decide. When New Hampshire ratified the Constitution on June 21, 1788, the U.S. Constitution technically should have become the law of the land. However, the states were aware that important states such as New York and Virginia had yet to ratify the document. Without these two important states, the system of government would have been on extremely shaky ground. Virginia, with a vote of eighty-nine to seventy-nine, ratified the Constitution on June 25. New York, by a razor-thin vote of thirty to twenty-seven and only because of Alexander Hamilton's passionate speeches during the ratifying convention (and helped by the fact that Virginia had recently ratified the Constitution), gave its approval on July 26, 1788. On March 4, 1789, the U.S. Constitution took effect and became the supreme law of the land.

Many states, especially Massachusetts, New York, and Virginia, only begrudgingly agreed to ratify the Constitution. Much of their concern stemmed from the fact that the Constitution had no bill of rights. The Bill of Rights comprises the first ten amendments to the U.S. Constitution. These amendments protect some of a citizen's most important rights and liberties: freedom of press, speech, religion, assembly, and petition (First Amendment); the right to a speedy trial (Sixth Amendment); and protection from cruel and unusual punishment (Eighth Amendment). Although Americans are often proud of these important rights, the original Constitution did not include any of these protections.

Many of the framers thought that a bill of rights would be unnecessary because the system created by the Constitution provided sufficient protection from abuse by the national government. Some, like Alexander Hamilton, believed that a bill of rights was not only unnecessary but was actively dangerous. He held that no bill of rights could list all of the rights and liberties that needed protection. Failing to list one of these rights or liberties might imply that that particular right or liberty was not protected. James Madison probably agreed with Hamilton, yet he also recognized the political necessity of adding a bill of rights. As a member of the House of Representatives, Madison played a central role in writing and shepherding the Bill of Rights through the first session of the House of Representatives. Since so many states made the adoption of a bill of rights a condition for their ratification of the Constitution, the Bill of Rights was quickly ratified by three-fourths of the states once two-thirds of the House and two-thirds of the Senate approved them. The Bill of Rights was adopted when Virginia ratified it on December 15, 1791. On March 1, 1792, Thomas Jefferson, America's first secretary of state, author of the Declaration of Independence, and a strong proponent of a Bill of Rights, officially announced that the Bill of Rights had been added to the U.S. Constitution.

The Ongoing History of the U.S. Constitution

There are various standards by which the U.S. Constitution might be judged. For some, the fact that this rather short document (of around 4,300 words) has lasted so long, despite the massive changes American society has experienced over the last two centuries, points to its power and importance. For others, the fact that so many nations have borrowed heavily from the U.S. Constitution for their own constitutions is a testament to the wisdom of adopting a federal system with separation of powers and checks and balances. For these reasons, it is not surprising that, for many Americans, the U.S. Constitution exists not simply as the blueprint for their system of government but also as a sacred document that together with the Declaration of Independence, serves as a testament to America's values and priorities as a nation.

The Constitution might also be judged on how well it addressed the goals that it set out for itself. The first part of the Constitution, the Preamble, is a list of goals that the framers wanted the Constitution to help America achieve. The Preamble reads, "We the People of the United States, in order to form a more perfect union, establish justice, insure domestic tranquillity, provide for the common defense, promote the general welfare, and secure the blessings of liberty to ourselves and our posterity, do ordain and establish this Constitution for the United States of America." This one sentence encapsulates well the elements that are essential to the foundation of the American system of government. First, by starting with the phrase "We the People of the United States," the Constitution creates a national citizenry in ways that the loose confederation of states under the Articles of Confederation could never do. Second, it clearly lays out the reasons for the Constitution ("to form a more perfect union," "provide for the common defense," etc.). Many of these are the wants and securities that the Articles of Confederation had been shown unable to provide. Finally, unlike the Declaration of Independence, which also expressed the nation's intentions and goals, the Preamble creates a government ("do ordain and establish this Constitution of the United States of America").

On May 26, 1987, two hundred years after the fifty-five delegates met to debate the U.S. Constitution in Philadelphia, the *New York Times* published a survey asking Americans how well they thought the U.S. Constitution did at addressing these goals articulated in its Preamble. Seventy-six percent of those polled felt that it had done a good job of "providing for the national defense." Seventy percent felt that it had done a good job of "making Americans think of themselves as part of one nation." Only a slim majority (53 percent) thought that it had done a good job of "establishing a fair system of justice." Finally, a minority (41 percent) believed that the U.S. Constitution had done a good job of "treating all people equally." The last item, equal treatment of all people, is only implicitly presented as a goal in the Preamble; however, the perception that the Constitution has not achieved this implicit goal suggests that many Americans believe that some work remains undone.

A final way of assessing the U. S. Constitution is to analyze the history of how a group of American patriots came together in Philadelphia for four months in the summer of 1787 to hammer out a new system of government. Studying that history reveals that many aspects of the U.S. Constitution represent an impressive advancement in the art and science of governing people while at the same time protecting citizens' rights and liberties. On the other hand, other components were adopted primarily as politically expedient compromises made by individuals interested in protecting personal and regional interests. (Slavery and the Three-Fifths Compromise were obvious examples of an issue that would continue to haunt the new nation.) Regardless of the means by which it is assessed, the U.S. Constitution is a remarkable document, with a remarkable history. Because of its continued importance to American government and society, it is also a history that continues well over two centuries after it was first conceived.

Notes

1. Quoted in Christopher Collier and James Lincoln Collier, *Decision in Philadelphia: The Constitutional Convention of 1787.* New York: Random House, 1986, p. 9.

2. Quoted in Kenneth Janda, Jeffrey Berry, and Jerry Goldman, *The Challenge of Democracy: Government in America,* 4th ed. Boston: Houghton Mifflin, 1995, p. 70.

3. Broadus Mitchell and Louise Pearson Mitchell, *A Biography of the Constitution of the United States: Its Origin, Formation, Adoption, Interpretation.* 2nd ed. New York: Oxford University Press, 1975, p. 6.

4. Jack Rakove, "The Road to Philadelphia, 1781–1787," in Leonard W. Levy and Dennis J. Mahoney, eds. *The Framing and Ratification of the Constitution.* New York: Macmillan, 1987, p. 101.

5. Clinton Rossiter, *1787: The Grand Convention.* New York: Macmillan, 1966, p. 50.

6. Richard Bernstein, with Kym Rice, *Are We to Be a Nation?* Cambridge, MA: Harvard University Press, 1987, p. 87.

7. Rakove, "The Road to Philadelphia, 1781–1787," p. 99.

8. Collier and Collier, *Decision in Philadelphia,* p. 13.

9. Quoted in Catherine Drinker Bowen, *Miracle at Philadelphia: The Story of the Constitutional Convention, May to September 1787.* Boston: Little, Brown, 1966, p. 13.

10. Quoted in Bernstein, *Are We to Be a Nation?* p. 167.

Chapter 1

Signs of a Failing System

Chapter Preface

E ven before the last state had ratified them in 1781, the Articles of Confederation had faced criticism. The critics, most prominently Alexander Hamilton, General George Washington's aide-de-camp in the Revolutionary War, thought that the country's first attempt at a government was too weak to deal with the internal and external problems that faced the young nation. Rather than a national government that could only do what the thirteen separate state governments allowed it to do, the critics of the Articles of Confederation suggested a stronger national government that would have the authority to negotiate treaties, regulate trade among the states, and have a source of independent funding. This would allow the government to act, at times, against the wishes of the various state governments when national emergencies required it to do so.

Not everyone thought that the Articles of Confederation were flawed, however. Many proponents liked a system of government with a weak central government and strong state governments. They feared that a strong national government would turn into a legislature like the British Parliament, from which they had just spent many years (1776–1781) attempting to extricate themselves. Supporters also approved of the Articles of Confederation because it allowed each state to make its own decisions without any input or interference from the national government. After the Declaration of Independence, each state wrote its own state constitution. States were not eager to change the way that they did things simply because a distant national government would find it more convenient.

This was the attitude of most people until the states learned the lesson that going it alone was not always in their best interest. This point was made most clearly by Shays's Rebellion of 1786. Facing an armed rebellion in the western part of Massachusetts by farmers who refused to pay their taxes, the Massachusetts legislature turned to the Confederation Congress for help. Congress agreed to send the national army to stop the rebellion. However, it was estimated to cost $530,000, and most of the other states refused to give any money for a problem that they felt was really only a concern for Massachusetts.

The importance of Shays's Rebellion is not that it seriously threatened the state government of Massachusetts. In fact, the rebellion was quickly suppressed, with little loss of life, when Massachusetts called on its own state militia in late January 1787. Instead, the importance of this incident was that it convinced some previous supporters of the Articles of Confederation that the current system was inadequate to deal with potentially devastating crises.

An Early Critique of the Articles of Confederation

Alexander Hamilton

> Not everyone approved of the system of government created by the Articles of Confederation. In this letter, written to his friend and a New York delegate to the Confederation Congress, James Duane, Alexander Hamilton discusses what he sees as the primary weaknesses of the Articles of Confederation. Hamilton believes that a strong central government—rather than a system that privileged state government power at the expense of a weak national government—was the only way for the new American nation to survive. This letter was dated September 3, 1780; therefore, it was written in the early stages of America's experience with the Articles of Confederation. However, many of Hamilton's theoretical concerns would become practical challenges only half a decade later during Shays' Rebellion of 1786–87. Alexander Hamilton served as General George Washington's aide-de-camp during the American Revolutionary war and would be a delegate to the Constitutional Convention in 1787 as well as a delegate to the New York state ratifying convention of 1788.

Agreeably to your request and my promise I sit down to give you my ideas of the defects of our present system and the changes necessary to save us from ruin. They may perhaps be the reveries of a projector rather than the sober

From Alexander Hamilton's letter of September 3, 1780, to James Duane, ALS, *The Hamilton Papers,* (Washington, DC: Library of Congress).

views of a politician. You will judge of them and make what use you please of them.

The fundamental defect is a want of power in Congress. It is hardly worth while to show in what this consists, as it seems to be universally acknowledged, or to point out how it has happened, as the only question is how to remedy it. It may, however, be said that it has originated from three causes. [First, there is] an excess of spirit of liberty which has made the particular states show a jealousy of all power not in their own hands; and [second] this jealousy has led them to exercise a right of judging in the last resort of the measures recommended by Congress, and of acting according to their own opinions of their propriety or necessity, a diffidence in Congress of their own powers, by which they have been timid and indecisive in their resolutions, constantly making concessions to the states, till they have scarcely left themselves the shadow of power. [Third, there is] a want of sufficient means at their disposal to answer the public exigencies and of vigor to draw forth those means, which have occasioned them to depend on the states individually to fulfil their engagements with the army, and the consequence of which has been to ruin their influence and credit with the army, [and] to establish its dependence on each state separately rather than *on them* (that is, rather than on the whole collectively).

Undefined Powers

It may be pleaded, that Congress had never any definitive powers granted them and of course could exercise none— could no nothing more than recommend. The manner in which Congress was appointed would warrant, and the public good required, that they should have considered themselves as vested with full power *to preserve the republic from harm.* They have done many of the highest acts of sovereignty, which were always cheerfully submitted to—the declaration of independence, the declaration of war, the levying an army, creating a navy, emitting money, making alliances with foreign powers, appointing a dictator, &c.

&c.—all these implications of a complete sovereignty were never disputed, and ought to have been a standard for the whole conduct of Administration. Undefined powers are discretionary powers, limited only by the object for which they were given—in the present case, the independence and freedom of America. The confederation made no difference; for as it has not been generally adopted, it had no operation. But from what I recollect of it, Congress have even descended from the authority which the spirit of that act gives them, while the particular states have no further attended to it than as it suited their pretensions and convenience. It would take too much time to enter into particular instances, each of which separately might appear inconsiderable, but united are of serious import. I only mean to remark, not to censure.

The States Have Too Much Authority

But the confederation itself is defective and requires to be altered; it is neither fit for war, nor peace. The idea of an uncontrolable sovereignty in each state, over its internal police, will defect the other powers given to Congress and make our union feeble and precarious. There are instances without number where acts necessary for the general good and which rise out of the powers given to Congress must interfere with the internal police of the states, and there are as many instances in which the particular states by arrangements of internal police can effectually though indirectly counteract the arrangements of Congress. You have already had examples of this for which I refer you to your own memory.

The confederation gives the states individually too much influence in the affairs of the army; they should have nothing to do with it. The entire formation and disposal of our military forces ought to belong to Congress. It is an essential cement of the union; and it ought to be the policy of Congress to destroy all ideas of state attachments in the army and make it look up wholly to them. For this purpose all appointments, promotions and provisions whatsoever ought to be made by them. It may be apprehended that this may be dangerous to liberty. But nothing appears more evident to me, than that we run much greater risk of having a weak and disunited federal government than one which will be able to usurp upon the rights of the people. Already some of the lines of the army would obey their states in opposition to Congress notwithstanding the pains we have taken to preserve the unity of the army— if any thing would hinder this it would be the personal

Alexander Hamilton

influence of the General [George Washington], a melancholy and mortifying consideration.

The forms of our state constitutions must always give them great weight in our affairs and will make it too difficult to bend them to the persuit of a common interest, too easy to oppose whatever they do not like and to form partial combinations subversive of the general one. There is a wide difference between our situation and that of an empire under one simple form of government, distributed into counties provinces or districts, which have no legislatures but merely magistratical bodies to execute the laws of a common sovereign. Here the danger is that the sovereign will have too much power to oppress the parts of which it is composed. In our case, that of an empire composed of confederated states each with a government completely organised within itself, having all the means to draw its subjects to a close dependence on itself—the danger is directly the reverse. It is that the common sovereign will not have power sufficient to unite the different members together, and direct the common forces to the interest and happiness of the whole. . . .

The confederation too gives the power of the purse too entirely to the state legislatures. It should provide perpetual funds in the disposal of Congress—by a land tax, poll tax, or the like. All imposts upon commerce ought to be laid by Congress and appropriated to their use, for without certain revenues, a government can have no power; that power, which holds the purse strings absolutely, must rule. This seems to be a medium, which without making Congress altogether independent will tend to give reality to its authority.

Another defect in our system is want of method and energy in the administration. This has partly resulted from the other defect, but in a great degree from prejudice and the want of a proper executive. Congress has kept the power too much into their own hands and have meddled too much with details of every sort. Congress is properly a deliberative corps and it forgets itself when it attempts to play the executive. It is impossible such a body, numerous as it is, constantly fluctuating, can ever act with sufficient decision, or with system. Two-thirds of the members, one-half of the time, cannot know what has gone before them or what connection the subject in hand has to what has been transacted on former occasions. The members, who have been more permanent, will only give information, that promotes the side they espouse, in the present case, and will as often mislead as enlighten. The variety of business must distract, and the proneness of every assembly to debate must at all times delay. . . .

Military Concerns

A third defect is the fluctuating constitution of our army. This has been a pregnant source of evil; all our military misfortunes, three-fourths of our civil embarrassments are to be ascribed to it. . . .

The imperfect and unequal provision made for the army is a fourth defect. . . . Without a speedy change the army must dissolve; it is now a mob, rather than an army, without clothing, without pay, without provision, without morals, without discipline. We begin to hate the country for its neglect of us; the country begins to hate us for our oppressions of them. Congress has long been jealous of us; we have now lost all confidence in them and give the worst construction to all they do. Held together by the slenderest ties, we are ripening for a dissolution.

The present mode of supplying the army—by state purchases—is not one of the least considerable defects of our system. It is too precarious a dependence, because the states will never be sufficiently impressed with our necessities. Each will make its own ease a primary object, the supply of the army a secondary one. The variety of channels through which the business is transacted will multiply the number of persons employed and the opportunities of embezzling public money. From the popular spirit on which most of the governments turn, the state agents, will be men of less character and ability, nor will there be so rigid a responsibility among them as there might easily be among those in the employ of the continent, of course not so much diligence care or economy. Very little of the money raised in the several states will go into the Continental treasury, on pretense that it is all exhausted in providing the quotas of supplies, and the public will be without funds for the other demands of governments. The expence will be ultimately much greater and the advantages much smaller. We actually feel the insufficiency of this plan and have reason to dread under it a ruinous extremity of want.

Potential Remedies

These are the principal defects in the present system that now occur to me. There are many inferior ones in the organization of particular departments and many errors of administration which might be pointed out; but the task would be troublesome and tedious, and if we had once remedied those I have mentioned, the others would not be attended with much difficulty.

I shall now propose the remedies, which appear to me applicable to our circumstances and necessary to extricate our affairs from their present deplorable situation.

The first step must be to give Congress powers competent to the public exigencies. . . . The confederation in my opinion should give Congress complete sovereignty; except as to that part of internal police, which relates to the rights of property and life among individuals and to raising money by internal taxes. It is necessary, that every thing, belonging to this, should be regulated by the state legislatures. Congress should have complete sovereignty in all that relates to war, peace, trade, finance, and to the management of foreign affairs; the right of declaring war, of raising armies, officering, paying them, directing their motions in every respect, of equipping fleets and doing the same with them, of building fortifications, arsenals, magazines, &c. &c., of making peace on such conditions as they think proper; of regulating trade, determining with what countries it shall be carried on, granting indulgencies laying prohibitions on all the articles of export or import, imposing duties granting bounties & premiums for raising, exporting, importing and applying to their own use the product of these duties, only giving credit to the states on whom they are raised in the general account of revenues and expences, instituting Admiralty courts, &c., of coining money, establishing banks on such terms, and with such privileges as they think proper, appropriating funds and doing whatever else relates to the operations of finance; transacting every thing with foreign nations, making alliances offensive and defensive, treaties of commerce, &c. &c. . . .

Another step of immediate necessity is to recruit the army for the war, or at least for three years. This must be done by a mode similar to that which is practiced in Sweden. There the inhabitants are thrown into classes of sixteen, and when the sovereign wants men each of these classes must furnish one. They raise a fixed sum of money, and if one of the class is willing to become a soldier, he receives the money and offers himself a volunteer; if none is found to do this, a draft is made, and he on whom the lot falls receives the money and is obliged to serve. The minds of the people are prepared for a thing of this kind; the heavy bounties they have been obliged to pay for men to serve a few months must have disgusted them with this mode and made them desirous of another, that will once for all answer the public purposes and obviate a repetition of the demand. It ought by all means to be attempted, and Congress should frame a general plan and press the execution upon the states. When the confederation comes to be framed, it ought to provide for this by a fundamental law, and hereafter there would be no doubt of the success. But we cannot now wait for this; we want to replace the men whose times of service will expire the 1st of January, for then, without this, we shall have no army remaining and the enemy may do what they please. . . .

Congress should endeavour, both upon their credit in Europe, and by every possible exertion in this country, to provide clothing for their officers, and should abolish the whole system of state supplies. . . . All other compensations to the army should be immediately taken up by Congress, and not left to the states. . . . The advantages of securing the attachment of the army to Congress, and binding them to the service by substantial ties are immense. We should then have discipline, an army in reality, as well as in name. Congress would then have a solid basis of authority and consequence, for to me it is an axiom that in our constitution an army is essential to the American union. . . .

Hopes for a Successful Convention

I have only skimmed the surface of the different subjects I have introduced. Should the plans recommended come into contemplation in earnest and you desire my further thoughts, I will endeavor to give them more form and particularity. I am persuaded a solid confederation [with] a permanent army [would have] a reasonable prospect of subsisting; it would give us treble [triple] consideration in Europe and produce a peace this winter.

If a Convention is called the minds of all the states and the people ought to be prepared to receive its determinations by sensible and popular writings, which should conform to the views of Congress. There are epochs in human affairs, when *novelty* even is useful. If a general opinion prevails that the old way is bad, whether true or false, and this obstructs or relaxes the operation of the public service, a change is necessary if it be but for the sake of change. This is exactly the case now. 'Tis an universal sentiment that our present system is a bad one, and that things do not go right on this account. The measure of a Convention would revive the hopes of the people and give a new direction to their passions, which may be improved in carrying points of substantial utility. The Eastern states have already pointed out this mode to Congress; they ought to take the hint and anticipate the others.

And, in future, My Dear Sir, two things let me recommend, as fundamental rules for the conduct of Congress—to attach the army to them by every motive, to maintain an air of authority (not domineering) in all their measures with the states. The manner in which a thing is done has more influence than is commonly imagined. Men are governed by opinion; this opinion is as much influenced by appearances as by realities; if a Government appears to be confident of its own powers, it is the surest way to inspire the same confidence in others; if it is diffident, it may be certain, there will be a still greater diffidence in others, and that its authority will not only be distrusted, controverted, but condemned.

I wish too Congress would always consider that a kindness consists as much in the manner as in the thing: the best things done hesitatingly and with an ill grace lose their effect, and produce disgust rather than satisfaction or gratitude. In what Congress has at any time done for the army, they have commonly been too late: They have seemed to yield to importunity rather than to sentiments of justice or to a regard to the accomodation of their troops. An attention to this idea is of more importance than it may be thought. I who have seen all the workings and progress of the present discontents, am convinced, that a want of this has not been among the most inconsiderable causes.

You will perceive, My Dear Sir, this letter is hastily written and with a confidential freedom, not as to a member of Congress, whose feelings may be sore at the prevailing clamours; but as to a friend who is in a situation to remedy public disorders, who wishes for nothing so much as truth, and who is desirous of information, even from those less capable of judging than himself.

Caution Against a Constitutional Convention

The Massachusetts Delegation to the Confederation Congress

In 1785, the Massachusetts legislature passed a resolution in favor of calling a convention to discuss changes to the Articles of Confederation. On September 3, 1785, the Massachusetts delegation to the Confederation Congress wrote a letter to the Massachusetts governor, James Bowdoin. In this letter, the delegates admit that there are important problems with the Articles of Confederation. However, they caution the governor and the legislature that calling a convention might not produce the results that Massachusetts desires. For example, they worry that such a convention might not even be legal under the Articles of Confederation. They also suggest that modest and temporary changes, rather than permanent constitutional amendments, might be a better solution to some of the problems. Most importantly, they worry that, while the Confederation Congress or the states could reject any changes in government proposed by the convention, rejecting the ideas of the most prominent politicians of the day would be difficult and would probably weaken the government.

It may be necessary . . . to observe that many are of opinion [that] the states have not yet had experience sufficient to determine the extent of powers vested in Congress by the Confederation, and therefore, that every measure at this time

From *Letters of Delegates to Congress, 1774–1789*, vol. 22, *November 1, 1784–November 6, 1785*, edited by Paul H. Smith (Washington, DC: Library of Congress, pp. 610–14).

proposing an alteration is premature. But admitting the necessity of immediately investing Congress with more commercial powers, it may be expedient to enquire.

Temporary Powers May Prove Best

First. Whether good policy does not require that those powers should be temporary? In determining this question, we are led to consider the commercial evils to be remedied, the efficacy of temporary powers for this purpose and the disposition of the several states touching the subject. The evils principally consist in the impositions, restrictions, and prohibitions of foreign powers on our Commerce and in the embarrassments resulting from the commercial regulations of our own states. How far temporary powers can remedy these evils, perhaps time and experience can only determine. Thus, much may nevertheless be suggested that, as the several treaties which are now negotiating by our commissioners in Europe are not to exceed the term of fifteen years, if the commercial powers to be vested in Congress should be of a similar duration, they may remedy the evils for that term. At the expiration thereof, a new commercial epoch will commence, when the states will have a more clear and comprehensive view of their commercial interests and the best means for promoting the same whether by treaties abroad or by the delegation and exercise of greater commercial powers at home. Whatever the disposition of the states may be, it can only be known by their acts. . . . The different views which they have had of the subject give reason to suppose that some legislatures will think temporary commercial powers elegible under present circumstances. Should this be the opinion of but one, an attempt immediately to delegate perpetual commercial powers must fail and may prevent a delegation of temporary powers—for in politics as in private life, by aiming at too much, we oft-times accomplish nothing.

Secondly. If the states are unanimously disposed to increase the commercial powers of the Confederacy, should not the additional powers, be in the first instance temporary, and the adoption of them as part of the Confederation depend on their beneficial effects? This is a question on which we propose not to venture a decided opinion; but experience teaches us, that in the formation of constitutions and laws, the wisest men have not been able to foresee the evasions and abuses, which in the operation have resulted from vague terms and expressions, latent inconsistencies, artful constructions and from too full and unguarded a delegation of powers. . . . The powers, once delegated in the Confederation cannot be revoked without the *unanimous consent* of the states. *This* may be earnestly sought for, but never obtained. The federal and state constitutions, are the great bulwarks of liberty. If they are subject, on trivial or even important occasions, to be revised and re-revised, altered & re-altered, they must cease to be considered as effectual & sacred barriers—and like landmarks frequently changed, [they] will afford no certain rule for ascertaining the boundaries, no criterion for distinguishing between the rights of government and those of the people. And, therefore, every alteration of the articles should be so thoroughly understood and digested as scarcely to admit the *possibility* of a disposition for a reconsideration.

Potential Loss of Public Confidence

Thirdly. Shall any alteration, either temporary or perpetual, be proposed in a way not *expressly* pointed out by the Confederation? The thirteenth article provides, "that the Articles of this Confederation shall be inviolably observed by every state, and the Union shall be perpetual; nor shall any alteration at any time hereafter be made in any of them: unless such alteration be agreed to in a Congress of the United States and be afterwards confirmed by the legislature of every state." Here, no provision is made, for or against a Convention, and therefore it may be said not to be inconsistent with this Article; but as the proceedings of a Convention would not be binding on Congress, should the latter think themselves under the necessity of rejecting the Report of the former, would not the States, after having thus incurred a considerable expence, be dissatisfied on the occasion? Would not the members of the Convention, who, it must be supposed, would be men of the first abilities and influence in the several States, be hurt and opposed in this instance to Congress? And would not parties, in the Legislatures and amongst the people be the consequence? If so, may not an apprehension of these evils have a tendency to influence some Members of Congress to give up their opinion respecting the report rather than to be considered as pertinacious and involved in contentions? And if such are the prospects of a Convention, will not Congress consider it as being contrary to the spirit of the Confederation? Indeed, we are doubtful, whether a measure of this kind would not be viewed as manifesting a want of confidence in Congress and, on this ground, meet their disapprobation.

Fourthly. If an alteration, either temporary or perpetual, of the commercial powers of Congress is to be considered by a Convention, shall the latter be authorized to revise the Confederation *generally* or only for express purposes? The great object of the Revolution, was the establishment of good government, and each of the states, in forming their own, as well as the federal Constitution, have adopted republican principles. Notwithstanding this, plans have been artfully laid and vigorously pursued, which, had they been successful, we think, would inevitably have changed our republican governments, into baleful aristocracies. . . .

Too Much Centralized Power?

What the effect then may be of calling a convention to revise the Confederation generally, we leave with your Excellency and the honorable legislature to determine. We are apprehensive, and it is our duty to declare it, that such a Measure would produce throughout the Union an exertion of the friends of an aristocracy to send members who would promote a change of government. We can form some judgment of the plan, which such members would report to Congress. But should the members be altogether republican, such have been the declamations of designing men against the Confederation generally—against the rotation of members, which perhaps is the best check to corruption and against the mode of altering the Confederation by the unanimous consent of the legislatures, which effectually prevents innovations in the Articles by intrigue or surprise—that we think there is great danger of [a] report which would invest Congress with powers that the honorable legislature have not the most distant intention to delegate. Perhaps it may be said, this can produce no ill effect because Congress may correct the Report however exceptionable, or if passed by them, any of the States may refuse to ratify it. True it is, that Congress and the States have such powers, but would not such a report, affect the tranquillity and weaken the government of the Union? We have already considered the operation of the report as it would respect Congress. If animosities and parties would naturally arise from their rejecting it, how much would these be increased, if the report approved by Congress and some of the states should be rejected by other states? Would there not be danger of a party spirit's being thus more generally diffused and warmly supported? Far distant we know it to be from the honorable legislature of Massachusetts to give up a single principle of republicanism, but when a general revision shall have proceeded from their motion and a report which to them may be highly offensive, shall have been confirmed by seven States in Congress and ratified by several Legislatures, will not these be ready to charge Massachusetts with inconsistency, in being the first to oppose a measure, which the state will be said to have originated? Massachusetts has great weight and is considered as one of the most republican states in the union. When it is known that the legislature has proposed a general revision, there can be no doubt that they will be represented as being convinced of the necessity of increasing generally the powers of Congress, and the opinion of the state will be urged with such art as to convince numbers that the Articles of the Confederation are altogether exceptionable. Thus, whilst measures are taken to guard against the evils arising from the want in one or two particulars of power in Congress, we are in great danger of incurring the other extreme. "More power in Congress" has been the cry from all quarters; but especially of those, whose veiws, not being confined to a government that will best promote the happiness of the people, are extended to one that will afford lucrative employments, civil and military. Such a government is an aristocracy, which would require a standing army and a numerous train of pensioners and placemen to prop and support its exalted administration. To recommend oneself to such an administration would be to secure an establishment for life and at the same time, to provide for his posterity. These are pleasing prospects which republican Governments do not afford. And it is not to be wondered at, that many persons of elevated views and idle habits in these states are desirous of the change. We are for increasing the power of Congress, as far as it will promote the happiness of the people; but at the same time are clearly of opinion that every measure should be avoided which would strengthen the hands of the enemies to a free government. An administration of the present Confederation with all its inconveniences is preferable to the risk of general dissentions and animosities which may approach to anarchy and prepare the way to a ruinous system of government.

Having thus, from a sense of the duty we owe to the United States as well as to our constituents, communicated to your Excellency, our sentiments on this important subject; we request you to lay them before the honorable legislature at their next session and to inform them that their measures for a general revision of the Confederation, if confirmed, shall be immediately communicated to Congress.

General Washington Worries About Shays's Rebellion

George Washington

After the Revolutionary War, George Washington, the former leader of the American army (and, thus, a national hero), had retired to his home, Mount Vernon, in Virginia. While primarily concerned with running his estate and directing his business interests, he maintained an interest in political affairs. In mid and late 1786, he became increasingly concerned over reports about growing unrest among farmers in western Massachusetts who suffered high taxes and other harsh economic conditions.

In two letters Washington describes the reasons for his concerns as the tensions turned toward a full-fledged rebellion led by an ex-soldier named Daniel Shays. In the first letter, written on August 1, 1786, to John Jay, the Secretary of Foreigner Affairs for America, Washington explains that he feels the rebellion reveals a profound weakness of the national legislature under the Articles of Confederation. He also is worried about rumors that some people had actually called for a return to a monarchy in the United States. In the second letter, written on November 5, 1786, to his friend James Madison, George Washington is able to report specifics about Shays's Rebellion because he had received information from his good friend, the Secretary of War, General Henry Knox.

From *The Writings of George Washington from the Original Manuscipt Sources, 1745–1799,* edited by John C. Fitzpatrick (Washington, DC: Government Printing Office, 1938).

[To John Jay]: Your sentiments, that our affairs are drawing rapidly to a crisis, accord with my own. What the event will be, is also beyond the reach of my foresight. We have errors to correct; we have probably had too good an opinion of human nature in forming our confederation. Experience has taught us, that men will not adopt and carry into execution measures the best calculated for their own good, without the intervention of a coercive power. I do not conceive we can exist long as a nation without having lodged somewhere a power, which will pervade the whole Union in as energetic a manner, as the authority of the state governments extends over the several states.

To be fearful of investing Congress, constituted as that body is, with ample authorities for national purposes, appears to me the very climax of popular absurdity and madness. Could Congress exert them for the detriment of the public, without injuring themselves in an equal or greater proportion? Are not their interests inseparably connected with those of their constituents? By the rotation of appointment, must they not mingle frequently with the mass of Citizens? Is it not rather to be apprehended, if they were possessed of the powers before described, that the individual members would be induced, to use them, on many occasions, very timidly and inefficaciously for fear of losing their popularity and future election? We must take human nature as we find it: perfection falls not to the share of mortals. Many are of opinion that Congress have too frequently made use of the suppliant humble tone of requisition, in applications to the States, when they had a right to assert their imperial dignity and command obedience. Be that as it may, requisitions are a perfect nihility where thirteen sovereign independent disunited States are in the habit of discussing and refusing compliance with them at their option. Requisitions are actually little better than a jest and a byword throughout the land. If you tell the legislatures they have violated the Treaty of Peace, and invaded the prerogatives of the confederacy, they will laugh in your face. What then is to be done? Things cannot go on in the same train forever. It is much to be feared, as you observe, that the better kind of people, being disgusted with the circumstances, will have their minds prepared for any revolution whatever. We are apt to run from one extreme into another. To anticipate and prevent disastrous contingencies would be the part of wisdom and patriotism.

What astonishing changes a few years are capable of producing. I am told that even respectable characters speak of a monarchical form of government without horror. From thinking proceeds speaking, thence to acting is often but a single step. But how irrevocable and tremendous! What a triumph for our enemies to verify their predictions! What a triumph for the advocates of despotism to find that we are incapable of governing ourselves, and that systems founded on the basis of equal liberty are merely ideal and fallacious! Would to God that wise measures may be taken in time to avert the consequences we have but too much reason to apprehend.

Retired as I am from the world, I frankly acknowledge I cannot feel myself an unconcerned spectator. Yet, having happily assisted in bringing the ship into port, and having been fairly discharged; it is not my business to embark again on a sea of troubles. Nor could it be expected, that my sentiments and opinions would have much weight on the minds of my countrymen; they have been neglected, though given as a last legacy in the most solumn manner. I had then perhaps some claims to public attention. I consider myself as having none at present. Mrs. Washington joins me in compliments, etc.

The Need for a Liberal and Energetic Constitution

[To James Madison]: Fain would I hope, that the great, and most important of all objects, the federal government, may be considered with that calm and deliberate attention which the magnitude of it so loudly calls for at this critical moment. Let prejudices, unreasonable jealousies, and local interest yield to reason and liberality. Let us look to our

As a young major, Washington was respected by his troops. In his later years he was an advocate of the new nation.

national character, and to things beyond the present period. No morn ever dawned more favourably than ours did, and no day was ever more clouded than the present! Wisdom, and good examples are necessary at this time to rescue the political machine from the impending storm. Virginia has now an opportunity to set the latter, and has enough of the former, I hope, to take the lead in promoting this great and arduous work. Without some alteration in our political creed, the superstructure we have been seven years raising at the expence of so much blood and treasure, must fall. We are fast verging to anarchy and confusion!

A letter which I have just received from General Knox, who had just returned from Massachusetts (whither he had been sent by Congress consequent of the commotion in that state) is replete with melancholy information of the temper, and designs of a considerable part of that people. Among other things he says,

> Their [Daniel Shays and his followers] creed is, that the property of the United States has been protected from confiscation of Britain by the joint exertions of *all* and therefore ought to be the *common property* of all. And he that attempts opposition to this

creed is an enemy to equity and justice and ought to be swept from off the face of the Earth.

again

They are determined to anihillate all debts public and private and have Agrarian Laws, which are easily effected by the means of unfunded paper money which shall be a tender in all cases whatever.

He adds

The numbers of these people amount in Massachusetts to about one fifth part of several populous counties, and to them may be collected, people of similar sentiments from the states of Rhode Island, Connecticut, and New Hampshire, so as to constitute a body of twelve or fifteen thousand desperate and unprincipled men. They are chiefly of the young and active part of the community.

How melancholy is the reflection, that in so short a space, we should have made such large strides towards fulfilling the prediction of our transatlantic foe! "leave them to themselves, and their government will soon dissolve." Will not the wise and good strive hard to avert this evil? Or will their supineness suffer ignorance, and the arts of self-interested designing disaffected and desperate characters, to involve this rising empire in wretchedness and contempt? What stronger evidence can be given of the want of energy in our governments than these disorders? If there exists not a power to check them, what security has a man for life, liberty, or property? To you, I am sure I need not add aught [more] on this subject. The consequences of a lax, or inefficient government, are too obvious to be dwelt on. Thirteen sovereignties pulling against each other, and all tugging at the federal head will soon bring ruin on the whole; whereas a liberal, and energetic Constitution, well guarded and closely watched, to prevent encroachments, might restore us to that degree of respectability and consequence, to which we had a fair claim, and the brightest prospect of attaining. With sentiments of the sincerest esteem etc.

A Prominent Woman Analyzes Shays's Rebellion

Abigail Adams

> Abigail Adams, the wife of the second President of the United States, John Adams, and the mother of the sixth President, John Quincy Adams, was a prolific and politically-astute letter writer. Her letters provide us with a wealth of firsthand information about the Revolutionary War and the first three decades of the American republic. In this letter, written to Thomas Jefferson on January 29, 1787, Abigail Adams provides her views on Shays's Rebellion. She believes that the farmers-turned-rebels are "ignorant, restless desperadoes, without conscience or principles." Although she did not support their cause, she remains hopeful that changes precipitated by the rebellion might strengthen the government.

With regard to the tumults in my native state which you inquire about, I wish I could say that report had exagerated them. It is too true, Sir, that they have been carried to so alarming a height as to stop the courts of justice in several counties. Ignorant, wrestless desperadoes, without conscience, or principles, have led a deluded multitude to follow their standard, under pretense of grievances which have no existence but in their imaginations. Some of them were

From Abigail Adams's letter of January 29, 1787, to Thomas Jefferson, as reprinted in *The Papers of Thomas Jefferson,* vol. 11, *1 January to 6 August 1787,* edited by Julian Boyd (Princeton, NJ: Princeton University Press, 1955).

crying out for a paper currency, some for an equal distribution of property, some were for annihilating all debts, others complaining that the Senate was a useless branch of government, that the court of common pleas was unnecessary, and that the sitting of the General Court in Boston was a grievance. By this list you will see the materials which compose this rebellion, and the necessity there is of the wisest and most vigorus measures to quell and suppress it. Instead of that laudable spirit which you approve, which makes a people watchfull over their liberties and alert in the defense of them, these mobish insurgents are for sapping the foundation, and destroying the whole fabric at once.

Examining the Causes May Benefit the Nation

But as these people make only a small part of the state, when compared to the more sensible and judicious, and although they create a just alarm and give much trouble and uneasiness, I cannot help flattering myself that they will prove salutary to the state at large, by leading to an investigation of the causes which have produced these commotions. Luxury and extravagance both in furniture and dress had pervaded all orders of our countrymen and women and were hastning fast to sap their independance by involving every class of citizens in distress and accumulating debts upon them which they were unable to discharge. Vanity was becoming a more powerfull principle than patriotism. The lower order of the community were pressed for taxes, and though possessed of landed property, they were unable to answer the demand, whilst those who possessed money were fearful of lending, lest the mad cry of the mob should force the legislature upon a measure very different from the touch of Midas.

By the papers I send you, you will see the beneficial effects already produced. An act of the legislature [was passed] laying duties of 15 per cent upon many articles of British manufacture and totally prohibiting others. A number of Volunteer lawyers, physicians and merchants from Boston made up a party of light horse commanded by Col.

Hitchbourn, Lt. Col. Jackson and Higgenson and went out in persuit of the insurgents and were fortunate enough to take three of their principal leaders, Shattucks, Parker and Page. Shattucks defended himself and was wounded in his knee with a broadsword. He is in jail in Boston and will no doubt be made an example of.

Putting Down the Rebellion

Benjamin Lincoln

> General Benjamin Lincoln was in a good position to describe
> the outcome of Shays's Rebellion because he was the com-
> mander of the Massachusetts militia responsible for defeating
> Daniel Shays and his followers. General Lincoln may not,
> however, be the most unbiased source of information about
> the rebels' demands. He, like many prominent and wealthy
> citizens of Massachusetts (and elsewhere), believes that
> Shays's Rebellion was primarily a way for lazy farmers to
> avoid paying their fair share of taxes and to get their debts
> wiped away by force. In these two letters to George Washing-
> ton, General Lincoln gives his analysis of the causes of
> Shays's Rebellion as well as a description of how the rebel-
> lion was put down. The first letter was written on December
> 4, 1786, during the middle of the crisis; the second letter was
> written on February 22, 1787, after Lincoln and his militia
> successfully defeated Daniel Shays and his followers, with
> very little loss of life on either side.

[December 4, 1786.]

What is the cause of all these commotions? The causes
are too many and too various for me to pretend to
trace and point them out. I shall therefore only mention
some of those which appear to be the principal ones. Among
those I may rank the ease with which property was acquired,
with which credit was obtained, and debts were discharged

Reprinted from *American History Told by Contemporaries,* vol. 3, *National Expansion,*
1783–1845, edited by Albert Bushnell Hart (New York: Macmillan, 1901).

in the time of the war. Hence people were diverted from their usual industry and economy. A luxuriant mode of living crept into vogue, and soon that income, by which the expenses of all should as much as possible be limited, was no longer considered as having any thing to do with the question at what expense families ought to live, or rather which they ought not to have exceeded. The moment the day arrived when all discovered that things were fast returning back into their original channels, that the industrious were to reap the fruits of their industry, and that the indolent and improvident would soon experience the evils of their idleness and sloth, very many startled at the idea, and instead of attempting to subject themselves to such a line of conduct, which duty to the public and a regard to their own happiness evidently pointed out, they contemplated how they should evade the necessity of reforming their system and of changing their present mode of life.

Debt Problems

They first complained of commutation, of the weight of public taxes, of the unsupportable debt of the Union, of the scarcity of money, and of the cruelty of suffering the private creditors to call for their just dues. This catalogue of complaints was listened to by many. County conventions were formed, and the cry for paper money, subject to depreciation, as was declared by some of their public resolves, was the clamor of the day. But notwithstanding instructions to members of the General Court and petitions from different quarters, the majority of that body were opposed to the measures. Failing of their point, the disaffected in the first place attempted, and in many instances succeeded, to stop the courts of law and to suspend the operations of government. This they hoped to do until they could by force sap the foundations of our constitution, and bring into the legislature creatures of their own by which they could mold a government at pleasure and make it subservient to all their purposes, and when an end should thereby be put to public and private debts, the agrarian law might follow with ease. In short, the want of industry, economy, and common honesty seem to be the causes of the present commotions.

It is impossible for me to determine when and how they will end as I see little probability that they will be brought to a period, and the dignity of government supported, without bloodshed. When a single drop is drawn, the most prophetic spirit will not, in my opinion, be able to determine when it will cease flowing. The proportion of debtors runs high in this State. Too many of them are against the government. The men of property and the holders of the public securities are generally supporters of our present constitution. Few of these have been in the field, and it remains quite problematical whether they will in time so fully discover their own interests as they shall be induced thereby to lend for a season part of their property for the security of the remainder. If these classes of men should not turn out on the broad scale with spirit, and the insurgents should take the field and keep it, our constitution will be overturned, and the federal government broken in upon by lopping off one branch essential to the well being of the whole. This cannot be submitted to by the United States with impunity. They must send force to our aid: when this shall be collected, they will be equal to *all* purposes. . . .

A Ploy to Delay Action

[February 22, 1787.] I had constant applications from committees and selectmen of the several towns in the Counties of Worcester and Hampshire, praying that the effusion of blood might be avoided; while the real design, as was supposed, of these applications was to stay our operations until a new court should be elected. They had no doubt if they could keep up their influence until another choice of the legislature and the executive that matters might be molded in General Court to their wishes. This to avoid was the duty of government. As all these applications breathed the same spirit, the same answer was given to them. . . .

In this position I remained refreshing the troops who had suffered very severe fatigue. This also gave time for the several towns to use their influence with their own people to return, if they thought proper to urge it, and to circulate among Shays' men that they would be recommended for a pardon if they would come in, and lay down their arms. The second of February I was induced to reconnoitre Shays' post on his right, left, and rear. I had received information by General Putnam before, that we could not approach him in front. I intended to have approached him on the third instance. This reconnoitering gave him an alarm. At three o'clock in the morning of the third, I received an application from Wheeler, that he wished to confer with General Putnam. His request was granted. He seemed to have no object but his personal safety. No encouragement being given him on this head, he returned a little after noon. In the evening of the same day, I was informed that Shays had left his ground, and had pointed his route towards Petersham in the County of Worcester, where he intended to make a stand as a number of towns in the vicinity had engaged to support him. Our troops were put in motion at eight o'clock. The first part of the night was pleasant, and the weather clement, but between two and three o'clock in the morning, the wind shifting to the westward, it became very cold and squally, with considerable snow. The wind immediately arose very high, and with the light snow which fell the day before and was falling, the paths were soon filled up; the men became fatigued and they were in part of the country where they could not be covered in the distance of eight miles, and the cold was so increased, that they could not halt in the road to refresh themselves. Under these circumstances they were obliged to continue their march. We reached Petersham about nine o'clock in the morning exceedingly fatigued with a march of thirty miles, part of it in a deep snow and in a most violent storm; when this abated, the cold increased and a great proportion of our men were frozen in some part or other, but none dangerously. We approached nearly the center of the town, where Shays had covered his men, and had we not been prevented from the steepness of a large hill at our entrance, and the depth of the snow, from throwing our men rapidly into it, we should have arrested very probably one half this force, for they were so surprized as it was that they had not time to call in their out-parties, or even their guards. About 150 fell into our hands, and none escaped but by the most precipitate flight in different directions.

This Business Is Accomplished

Thus, that body of men, who were a few days before offering the grossest insults to the best citizens of the Commonwealth and were menacing even government itself, were now nearly dispersed, without the shedding of blood but in an instance or two where the insurgents rushed on their own destruction. That so little has been shed is owning in a measure to the patience and obedience, the zeal and the fortitude in our troops, which would have done honor to veterans. A different line of conduct which Shays flattered his troops would have been followed, would have given them support and led them to acts of violence, whilst it must have buoyed up the hopes of their abettors, and stimulated them to greater exertions. . . .

. . . I at once threw detachments into different parts of the County, for the purpose of protecting the friends to government and apprehending those who had been in arms against it. This business is pretty fully accomplished, and there are no insurgents together in arms in the State.

Chapter 2

The Workings of the Convention

Chapter Preface

James Madison, on every day of the nearly four months that the convention lasted, placed himself in the center of the room, well-positioned to take notes on the proceedings. He was not the official secretary of the convention; however, the official secretary, Major William Jackson, accepted the job for the money that it paid him. Major Jackson did a lackluster job, so subsequent generations are thankful that Madison took it upon himself to take notes on the debates. Other delegates also provide insight into the personalities of the various delegates. For example, a Georgia delegate, William Pierce, included with his report to the Georgia legislature character sketches of the participants and observations about how debates were conducted.

More than the personalities of the delegates, however, the Constitutional Convention was influenced by its structure. Thirty members would attend an average session, thereby making it more akin to a committee meeting, where everyone who wished to participate could contribute directly, rather than a convention, where only a small percentage could be heard. Even so, some delegates, like Robert Morris, never spoke. Some, like Benjamin Franklin, would write out their thoughts in advance and have a fellow delegate read their statements to the convention. Others spoke often. For example, Alexander Hamilton, Gouverneur Morris, and James Madison each spoke well over one hundred separate times during the convention.

Voting was taken by states. Delaware, the nation's smallest state, insisted on this. They announced on the first day of the convention that they would leave the convention rather than surrender the one-state, one-vote rule. This would foreshadow one of the more important debates of the convention: determining how states would be allocated seats in the new legislature.

All deliberations were held in absolute secrecy until the convention completed its work. Secrecy had several benefits. First, it eliminated the possibility that the public would worry about provisions that would not actually make it into the final document. Second, enemies of the Constitutional Convention would use anything to create public fervor against the Constitution. By not allowing anyone to hear anything about the document until it was finished, the delegates did not provide outsiders the opportunity to stir up opposition. Third, secrecy freed the delegates to speak (and to change) their minds and to ponder different ideas without fear of public criticism. One unfortunate aspect of secrecy was that it did not provide the delegates any way to release the strong emotions that the debates would often create except in the debates themselves. However, this does make the debates rather interesting to read.

One important decision was the delegates' unanimous selection of George Washington as the president of the convention. The delegates were so sure of their choice that they broke the secrecy rule to let it be known publicly that they had chosen General Washington, the popular hero of the American Revolutionary War, to preside over the Constitutional Convention. Historians Broadus Mitchell and Louise Pearson Mitchell believe that "the fact that all was being done under Washington's eye was in itself enough to confer confidence."

Preparations for the Convention

George Mason

> The Constitutional Convention got a late start. It was sched-
> uled to begin on May 14, 1787, but the delegates could not
> begin work until May 25, 1787, when a quorum of seven
> states had arrived in Philadelphia. This letter, from George
> Mason to his son, George Mason Jr., dated May 20, 1787,
> describes what the delegates who arrived on time did while
> they waited for enough delegations to arrive. It also reveals
> one delegate's hopes that, despite obvious barriers to agree-
> ment among the various states, compromises could be made,
> and the weaknesses of the Articles of Confederation would
> be remedied.

Upon our arrival here on Thursday evening, I found only
the states of Virginia and Pennsylvania fully represented; and there are at this time only five—New York, the
two Carolinas, and the two before mentioned. All the states,
Rhode Island excepted, have made their appointments; but
the members drop in slowly. Some of the deputies from the
eastern states are here, but none of them have yet a sufficient
representation, and it will probably be several days before
the convention will be authorized to proceed to business.
The expectations & hopes of all the Union center in this
convention. God grant that we may be able to concert effectual means of preserving our country from the evils
which threaten us.

From George Mason's letter of May 20, 1787, to George Mason Jr., as reprinted in *The Papers of George Mason, 1725–1792,* vol. 3, *1787–1792,* edited by Robert A. Rutland (Chapel Hill: University of North Carolina Press, 1970).

The Virginia deputies (who are all here) meet and confer together two or three hours every day in order to form a proper correspondence of Sentiments. For form's sake, to see what new Deputies are arrived, & to grow into some Acquaintance with each other, we regularly meet every Day at 3 o'clock p.m. at the Statehouse. These and some occasional conversations with the deputies of different states and with some of the General Officers of the late Army are the only opportunities I have hither to had of forming my opinion upon the great subject of our mission, and consequently [it is] a very imperfect and indecisive one.

Hopes of Positive Change

Yet, upon the great principles of it, I have reason to hope there will be greater unanimity and less opposition, except from the little states, than was at first apprehended. The most prevalent idea, in the principal states seems to be a total alteration of the present federal system and substituting a great National Council, or Parliament, consisting of two branches of the legislature, founded upon the principles of equal proportionate representation, with full legislative powers upon all the objects of the Union; and an Executive: and to make the several state legislatures subordinate to the national, by giving the latter the power of a negative upon all such laws, as they shall judge contrary to the interest of the federal union. It is easy to foresee that there will be much difficulty in organizing a government upon this great scale, and at the same time reserving to the state legislatures a sufficient portion of power for promoting and securing the prosperity and happiness of their respective citizens. Yet, with a proper degree of coolness, liberality and candor (very rare commodities by-the-by) I doubt not but it may be effected. There are, among a variety, some very eccentric opinions upon this great subject, and what is a very extraordinary phenomenon, we are likely to find the republicans, on this occasion, issue from the southern & middle states, & the anti-republicans from the eastern. However extraordinary this may at first seem; it may, I think, be accounted for, from a very common & natural impulse of the human mind. Men, disappointed in expectations too hastily, and sanguinely formed, tired and disgusted with the unexpected evils they have experienced and anxious to remove them as far as possible, are very apt to run into the opposite extreme; and the people of the eastern states, setting out with more republican principles, have consequently been more disappointed than we have been.

Character Sketches of the Framers

William Pierce

While several delegates to the Constitutional Convention took notes on the proceedings, William Pierce, a Georgia delegate, is one of the few who describes more than the substantive debates that transpired. William Pierce's notes include descriptions of the delegates themselves. These character sketches analyze their appearance, speaking ability, intelligence, and personal style. Most of the time, Pierce attempts to emphasize the individual's positive attributes, but he is not entirely unwilling to criticize apparent faults.

From Massachusetts

MR. [RUFUS] KING is a man much distinguished for his eloquence and great parliamentary talents. He was educated in Massachusetts and is said to have good classical as well as legal knowledge. He has served for three years in the Congress of the United States with great and deserved applause, and is at this time high in the confidence and approbation of his countrymen. This gentleman is about thirty-three years of age, about five feet ten inches high, well formed, a handsome face, with a strong expressive eye, and a sweet high-toned voice. In his public speaking there is something peculiarly strong and rich in his expression, clear, and convincing in his arguments, rapid and irresistible at times in his eloquence, but he is not always equal. His action is natural, swimming, and graceful, but there is a rudeness

Reprinted from "Notes of William Pierce on the Federal Convention of 1787," *The American Historical Review,* vol. 3, January 1898, pp. 325–34.

of manner sometimes accompanying it. But take him *tout en- semble,* [altogether] he may with propriety be ranked among the luminaries of the present age.

MR. [NATHANIEL] GORHAM is a merchant in Boston, high in reputation, and much in the esteem of his countrymen. He is a man of very good sense, but not much improved in his education. He is eloquent and easy in public debate, but has nothing fashionable or elegant in his style; all he aims at is to convince, and where he fails it never is from his auditory not understanding him, for no man is more perspicuous and full. He has been President of Congress, and three years a member of that body. Mr. Gorham is about 46 years of age, rather lusty and has an agreable and pleasing manner.

MR. [ELBRIDGE] GERRY'S character is marked for integrity and perseverance. He is a hesitating and laborious speaker; [he] possesses a great degree of confidence and goes extensively into all subjects that he speaks on, without respect to elegance or flower of diction. He is connected and sometimes clear in his arguments, conceives well, and cherishes as his first virtue, a love for his country. Mr. Gerry is very much of a gentleman in his principles and manners; he has been engaged in the mercantile line and is a Man of property. He is about 37 years of age. . . .

From Connecticut

DR. [SAMUEL] JOHNSON is a character much celebrated for his legal knowledge; he is said to be one of the first classics in America, and certainly possesses a very strong and enlightened understanding.

As an orator in my opinion, there is nothing in him that warrants the high reputation which he has for public speaking. There is something in the tone of his voice not pleasing to the ear, but he is eloquent and clear—always abounding with information and instruction. He was once employed as an agent for the state of Connecticut to state her claims to certain landed territory before the British House of Commons; this office he discharged with so much dignity and made such an ingenious display of his powers that he laid the foundation of a reputation which will probably last much longer than his own life. Dr. Johnson is about sixty years of age, possesses the manners of a gentleman and engages the hearts of men by the sweetness of his temper and that affectionate style of address with which he accosts his acquaintance.

MR. [ROGER] SHERMAN exhibits the oddest shaped character I ever remember to have met with. He is awkward, unmeaning, and unaccountably strange in his manner. But in his train of thinking there is something regular, deep, and comprehensive; yet the oddity of his address, the vulgarisms that accompany his public speaking and that strange New England cant which runs through his public as well as his private speaking make everything that is connected with him grotesque and laughable, and yet he deserves infinite praise—no man has a better heart or a clearer head. If he cannot embellish, he can furnish thoughts that are wise and useful. He is an able politician, and extremely artful in accomplishing any particular object; it is remarked that he seldom fails. I am told he sits on the bench in Connecticut, and is very correct in the discharge of his judicial functions. In the early part of his life he was a shoemaker, but despising the lowness of his condition, he turned almanac maker and so progressed upwards to a judge. He has been several years a Member of Congress, and discharged the duties of his office with honor and credit to himself and advantage to the state he represented. He is about 60. . . .

From New York

COL. [ALEXANDER] HAMILTON is deservedly celebrated for his talents. He is a practitioner of the law, and reputed to be a finished scholar. To a clear and strong judgment he unites the ornaments of fancy, and whilst he is able, convincing and engaging in his eloquence, the heart and head sympathize in approving him. Yet there is something too feeble in his voice to be equal to the strains of oratory; it is my opinion that he is rather a convincing Speaker, [than] a blazing orator. Col. Hamilton requires time to think—he enquires into every part of his subject with the searchings of philosophy, and when he comes forward he comes highly charged with interesting matter; there is no skimming over the surface of a subject with him; he must sink to the bottom to see what foundation it rests on. His language is not always equal, sometimes didactic, . . . at others light and tripping. . . . His eloquence is not so defusive as to trifle with the senses, but he rambles just enough to strike and keep up the attention. He is about 33 years old, of small stature, and lean. His manners are tinctured with stiffness, and sometimes with a degree of vanity that is highly disagreeable. . . .

MR. [JOHN] LANSING is a practicing attorney at Albany, and Mayor of that corporation. He has a hisitation in his speech, that will prevent his being an orator of any eminence. His legal knowledge I am told is not extensive, nor his education a good one. He is, however, a man of good sense, plain in his manners, and sincere in his friendships. He is about 32 years of age.

From New Jersey

GOVERNOR [WILLIAM] LIVINGSTON is confessedly a man of the first rate talents, but he appears to me rather to indulge a sportiveness of wit than a strength of thinking. He is, however, equal to anything, from the extensiveness of his education and genius. His writings teem with satire and a neatness of style. But he is no orator and seems little acquainted with the guiles of policy. He is about 60 years old and remarkably healthy. . . .

MR. [WILLIAM] PATTERSON is one of those kind of men whose powers break in upon you, and create wonder and astonishment. He is a man of great modesty, with looks that bespeak talents of no great extent,—but he is a classic [scholar], a lawyer and an orator;—and of a disposition so favorable to his advancement that every one seemed ready to exalt him with their praises. He is very happy in the choice of time and manner of engaging in a debate, and never speaks but when he understands his subject well. This gentleman is about 34 years of age, of a very low stature. . . .

From Pennsylvania

DR. [BENJAMIN] FRANKLIN is well known to be the greatest philosopher of the present age; all the operations of nature he seems to understand—the very heavens obey him, and the clouds yield up their lightning to be imprisoned in his rod. But what claim he has to the politician, posterity must determine. It is certain that he does not shine much in public council—he is no speaker, nor does he seem to let politics engage his attention. He is, however, a most extraordinary man and tells a story in a style more engaging than anything I ever heard. Let his biographer finish his character. He is 82 years old and possesses an activity of mind equal to a youth of 25 years of age. . . .

MR. GOVERNEUR MORRIS is one of those geniuses in whom every species of talents combine to render him conspicuous and flourishing in public debate. He winds through all the mazes of rhetoric, and throws around him such a glare that he charms, captivates, and leads away the senses of all who hear him. With an infinite stretch of fancy he brings to view things when he is engaged in deep argumentation that render all the labor of reasoning easy and pleasing. But with all these powers he is fickle and inconstant—never pursuing one train of thinking, nor ever regular. He has gone through a very extensive course of reading, and is acquainted with all the sciences. No man has more wit, nor can any one engage the attention more than Mr. Morris. He was bred to the law, but I am told he disliked the profession, and turned merchant.

Gouverneur Morris

He is engaged in some great mercantile matters with his namesake Mr. Robert Morris. This gentleman is about 38 years old; he has been unfortunate in losing one of his legs and getting all the flesh taken off his right arm by a scald when a youth. . . .

From Maryland

MR. [LUTHER] MARTIN was educated for the Bar and is Attorney General for the state of Maryland. This Gentleman possesses a good deal of information, but he has a very bad delivery and [is] so extremely prolix [wordy] that he never speaks without tiring the patience of all who hear him. He is about 34 years of age. . . .

From Virginia

GENERAL [GEORGE] WASHINGTON is well known as the Commander-in-Chief of the late American Army. Having conducted these States to independence and peace, he now appears to assist in framing a government to make the people happy. Like Gustavus Vasa, he may be said to be the deliverer of his country; like Peter the Great, he appears as the politician and the statesman, and like Cincinnatus, he returned to his farm perfectly contented with being only a plain citizen, after enjoying the highest honor of the confederacy—and now only seeks for the approbation of his countrymen by being virtuous and useful. The General was conducted to the Chair as President of the Convention by the unanimous voice of its members. He is in the 52nd year of his age. . . .

MR. [GEORGE] MASON is a Gentleman of remarkable strong powers, and possesses a clear and copious understanding. He is able and convincing in debate, steady and firm in his principles and undoubtedly one of the best politicians in America. Mr. Mason is about 60 years old, with a fine strong constitution.

MR. [JAMES] MADISON is a character who has long been in public life, and what is very remarkable [is that] every person seems to acknowledge his greatness. He blends together the profound politician, with the scholar. In the management of every great question he evidently took the lead in the Convention, and though he cannot be called an orator, he is a most agreeable, eloquent, and convincing speaker. From a spirit of industry and application which he possesses in a most eminent degree, he always comes forward the best informed man of any point in debate. The affairs of the United States, he perhaps, has the most correct knowledge of, of any man in the Union. He has been twice a Member of Congress, and was always thought one of the ablest members that ever sat in that council. Mr. Madison is about 37 years of age, a gentleman of great modesty—with a remarkable sweet temper. He is easy and unreserved among his acquaintance and has a most agreable style of conversation. . . .

MR. [EDMUND] RANDOLPH is Governor of Virginia,—a young gentleman in whom unite all the accomplishments of the scholar, and the statesman. He came forward with the postulata, or first principles, on which the Convention acted, and he supported them with a force of eloquence and reasoning that did him great honor. He has a most harmonious voice, a fine person and striking manners. Mr. Randolph is about 32 years of age. . . .

From North Carolina

MR. [WILLIAM] BLOUNT is a character strongly marked for integrity and honor. He has been twice a Member of Congress, and in that office discharged his duty with ability and faithfulness. He is no speaker, nor does he possess any of those talents that make men shine—he is plain, honest, and sincere. Mr. Blount is about 36 years of age.

MR. [RICHARD DOBBS] SPAIGHT is a worthy man, of some abilities and fortune. Without possessing a genius to render him briliant, he is able to discharge any public trust that his country may repose in him. He is about 31 years of age.

MR. [HUGH] WILLIAMSON is a gentleman of education and talents. He enters freely into public debate from his close attention to most subjects, but he is no orator. There is a great degree of good humor and pleasantry in his character and in his manners there is a strong trait of the gentleman. He is about 48 years of age. . . .

From South Carolina

MR. CHARLES PINCKNEY is a young gentleman of the most promising talents. He is, although only 24 years of age, in possession of a very great variety of knowledge. Government, law, history and philosophy are his favorite studies, but he is intimately acquainted with every species of polite learning and has a spirit of application and industry beyond most men. He speaks with great neatness and perspicuity, and treats every subject as fully, without running into prolixity, as it requires. He has been a Member of Congress and served in that body with ability and eclat [brilliant success]. . . .

From Georgia

MR. [ABRAHAM] BALDWIN is a gentleman of superior abilities, and joins in a public debate with great art and eloquence. Having laid the foundation of a complete classical education at Harvard College, he pursues every other study with ease. He is well acquainted with books and characters and has an accomodating turn of mind, which enables him to gain the confidence of men and to understand them. He is a practising attorney in Georgia, and has been twice a Member of Congress. Mr. Baldwin is about 38 years of age. . . .

My own character I shall not attempt to draw, but leave those who may choose to speculate on it to consider it in any light that their fancy or imagination may depict. I am conscious of having discharged my duty as a soldier through the course of the late revolution with honor and propriety, and my services in Congress and the Convention were bestowed with the best intention towards the interest of Georgia and towards the general welfare of the Confederacy. I possess ambition, and it was that, and the flattering opinion which some of my friends had of me, that gave me a seat in the wisest council in the world and furnished me with an opportunity of giving these short sketches of the characters who composed it.

A Convention Update for an Interested Bystander

Edward Carrington

From 1785–1789, Thomas Jefferson, the writer of the Declaration of Independence, was the United States' ambassador to France. He relied on letters from friends, relatives, politicians, and others who were in America at the time to keep him abreast of the most pressing political events. In this letter, sent June 9, 1787, Edward Carrington, a Virginia delegate to the Confederation Congress from 1786–1788, writes to Thomas Jefferson, reporting to him what he can about the early days of the Constitutional Convention. As Edward Carrington was in New York, where the Confederation Congress met, he is unable to provide Jefferson with a detailed account of the Constitutional Convention which was meeting in Philadelphia. In his letter, Carrington makes several observations. The two most notable are his reference to the secrecy which surrounded the Constitutional Convention, and his warning to Thomas Jefferson that Jefferson might not approve of the direction taken by the convention. He gently reminds Jefferson that Jefferson had not been in the United States for several years and, thus, was not aware of the serious weaknesses of the Articles of Confederation.

The proposed scheme of a convention has taken more general effect and promises more solid advantages than was at first hoped for. All the States have elected representatives

From Edward Carrington's June 9, 1787, letter to Thomas Jefferson, as reprinted in *Documentary History of the Constitution of the United States of America, 1786–1870* (Washington, DC: U.S. Department of State, 1905).

except Rhode Island, whose apostasy [abandonment] from every moral, as well as political, obligation, has placed her perfectly without the views of her confederates; nor will her absence, or nonconcurrence, occasion the least impediment in any stage of the intended business. On Friday the 25th [May 1787] seven states having assembled at Philadelphia, the Convention was formed by the election of General Washington President. . . . The numbers have since increased to 11 states—New Hampshire has not yet arrived, but is daily expected.

The commissions of these gentlemen go to a thorough reform of our confederation—some of the states, at first, restricted their deputies to commercial objects, but have since liberated them. The latitude thus given, together with the generality of the commission from the states, have doubtless operated to bring General Washington forward, contrary to his more early determination. His conduct in both instances indicate a deep impression upon his mind of the necessity of some material change. It belongs to his wisdom and weight of character to be averse to meddling in a fruitless attempt, and this must have been the case upon a confined ground, or a very partial representation of the States; it would have been equally inconsistent with his situation to come forward upon any occasion, except in the extremity of public necessity. In every public act he hazards, without a possibility of gaining, reputation. He already possesses everything to be derived from the love or confidence of a free people, yet it seems that it remained for himself to add a luster to his character, by this patriotic adventure of all, for his country's good alone.

A Need for Change

The importance of this event is every day growing in the public mind, and it will, in all probability, produce an happy era in our political existence. Taking a view of the circumstances which have occasioned our calamities and the present state of things and opinions, I am flattered with this prospect—public events in the United States since the peace have given a cast to the American character, which is by no means its true countenance. Delinquencies of the States in their federal obligations, acts of their legislatures violating public treaties and private contracts, and an universal imbecility in the public administrations, it is true, form the great features of our political conduct; but [these] have resulted rather from constitutional defects, and accidental causes than the natural dispositions of the people. Destitute as the federal sovereignty is of coercive principle, backwardness in the component parts to comply with its recommendations, is natural and inevitable. Coercion in government produces a double effect. While it compels the obedience of the refractory, it redoubles the alertness of the virtuous by inspiring a confidence in the impartiality of its burdens. From defect of penalty, ideas of delinquency are inseparable. States, as well as individuals, will contemplate both together, and apprehensions of unequal performance, produce disgust and apathy throughout.

The nefarious acts of state governments have proceeded not from the will of the people. Peace once obtained, men whose abilities and integrity had gained the entire popular confidence, whose zeal, or indolence, in the public affairs, alike, moved, or lulled, the people, retired from the busy scene or at least acted with indifference. The newspapers ceased to circulate with public information. Demagogues of desperate fortunes, mere adventurers in fraud, were left to act unopposed. Their measures, of course, either obtained the consent of the multitude, by misrepresentation, or assumed the countenance of popularity because none said nay—hence have proceeded paper money, breaches of treaty, etc. The ductility of the multitude is fully evidenced in the case of the late tumults in Massachusetts [Shays' Rebellion]. Men who were of good property and owed not a shilling were involved in the train of desperados to suppress the courts. A full representation of the public affairs from the General Court through the clergy has reclaimed so great a proportion of the deluded that a rebellion which a few months ago threatened the subversion of the government is, by measures scarsely deserving the name of exertion, suppressed, and one decided act of authority would eradicate it forever. In this experement it is proved that full intelligence of the public affairs not only would keep the people right but will set them so after they have got wrong.

The People Will Support a Strong Government

Civil liberty, in my opinion, never before took up her residence in a country so likely to afford her a long and grateful protection as the United States. A people more generally enlightened than any other under the sun, and in the habits of owning, instead of being mere tenants in, the soil, must be proportionally alive to her sacred rights and qualified to guard them; and I am persuaded that the time is fast approaching when all these advantages will have their fullest influence. Our tendency to anarchy and consequent despotism is felt, and the alarm is spreading. Men are brought into action who had consigned themselves to an eve of rest, and the Convention, as a beacon, is rousing the attention of the Empire.

The prevailing impression, as well in as out of [the] Convention, is that a federal government adapted to the permanent circumstances of the country, without respect to the habits of the day, be formed, whose efficiency shall pervade the whole Empire. It may, and probably will, at first, be viewed with hesitation, but, derived and patronsed as it will be, its influence must extend into a general adoption as the present fabric gives way. That the people are disposed to be governed is evinced in their turning out to support the shadows under which they now live, and if a work of wisdom is prepared for them, they will not reject it to commit themselves to the dubious issue of anarchy.

The Issues of Debate

The debates and proceedings of the Convention are kept in profound secrecy. Opinions of the probable result of their deliberations can only be formed from the prevailing impressions of men of reflection and understanding. These are reducible to two schemes: the first, a consolidation of the whole Empire into one republic, leaving in the states nothing more than subordinate courts for facilitating the administration of the laws; the second an investiture of federal sovereignty with full and independant authority as to the trade, revenues, and forces of the Union, and the rights of peace and war, together with a negative upon all the acts of the state legislatures. The first idea, I apprehend, would be impracticable and, therefore, do not suppose it can be adopted. General laws through a country embracing so many climates, productions, and manners as the United States, would operate many oppressions, and a general legislature would be found incompetent to the formation of local ones, as a majority would, in every instance, be ignorant of, and unaffected by, the objects of legislation. The essential rights, as well as advantages, of representation would be lost, and obedience to the public decrees could only be ensured by the exercise of powers different from those derivable from a free constitution. Such an experement must therefore terminate in a despotism, or the same inconveniences we are now deliberating to remove. Something like the second will probably be formed. Indeed, I am certain that nothing less than what will give the federal sovereignty a complete control over the state governments, will be thought worthy of discussion. Such a scheme constructed upon well adjusted principles would certainly give us stability and importance as a nation, and if the Executive powers can be sufficiently checked, must be eligible. Unless the whole has a decided influence over the parts, the constant effort will be to resume the delegated powers, and there cannot be an inducement in the federal sovereignty to refuse its assent to an innocent act of a state. The negative which the King of England had upon our Laws was never found to be materially inconvenient.

Prepare for the Outcome

The ideas here suggested are far removed from those which prevailed when you were amongst us, and as they have arisen with the most able, from an actual view of events, it is probable you may not be prepared to expect them. They are however the most moderate of any which obtain in any general form amongst reflective and intelligent men. The Eastern opinions are for a total surrender of the state sovereignties, and, indeed, some amongst them go to a monorchy at once. They have verged to anarchy, while to the southward we have only felt an inconvenience, and their proportionate disposition to an opposite extreme is a natural consequence.

I have encroached on your patience by a long letter, nor could I compress the information which I wished to convey into a smaller compass. Disquisition has been avoided except where it became necessary to complete my ideas, because, being possessed of facts and circumstances your own reflections will furnish better, and it will afford me pleasure, as well as improvement, to receive them from you.

Rumors from Outside the Convention

David Humphreys

> Extreme secrecy of the negotiations during the convention
> was demanded by the prominent leaders at the Constitutional
> Convention, especially by George Washington, who was
> unanimously elected the Convention president. This letter,
> from David Humphreys, an aide-de-camp to General Wash-
> ington during the Revolutionary War, to his friend and fellow
> aide-de-camp, Alexander Hamilton, illustrates the negative
> impact that secrecy had. Humphreys reports the closed-door
> policy encouraged wild speculation concerning the intents
> of the convention. Whether a sincere wish to return to monar-
> chy or a political ploy to scare Antifederalists into supporting
> a stronger national government, a rumor was spreading that
> British king George III's second son would be made the king
> of the United States.

Our friend Col. Wadsworth has communicated to me a
letter in which you made inquiries respecting a political letter that has lately circulated in this state. I arrived in
this town yesterday [August 31, 1787] and have since con-
versed with several intelligent persons on the subject. It appears to have been printed in a Fairfield paper as long ago
as the 25th of July. I have not been able to trace it to its
source. Mr. [Hezekiah] Wetmore informs me that when he
first saw this letter it was in the hands of one Jared Mans-
field, who, I believe, has formerly been reputed a Loyalist
[to England's monarchy]. Indeed, it seems to have been
received and circulated with avidity by that class of people,

From David Humphreys's September 1, 1787, letter to Alexander Hamilton, ALS, *The
Hamilton Papers* (Washington, DC: Library of Congress).

whether it was fabricated by them or not. I think, however, there is little doubt that it was manufactured in this state. I demanded of Mr. Wetmore what he thought were the wishes and objects of the writer of that letter; he said he believed it might be written principally for the amusement of the author and perhaps with some view to learn whether the people were not absolutely indifferent to all government and dead to all political sentiment.

Before I saw the letter in question, a paragraph had been published by Mr. [Josiah] Meigs, giving an account of it and attempting to excite the apprehension of the Antifederalists, with an idea, that the most disastrous consequences are to be expected, unless we shall accept the proceedings of the convention. Some think this was the real design of that fictitious performance; but others, with more reasons, [think] that it was intended to feel the public pulse and to discover whether the

Secrecy and the Constitutional Convention

Secrecy throughout the Constitutional Convention was demanded of all delegates. In fact, James Madison, refused to tell even his own father the most mundane details about the Convention. University of Cincinnati historian, John Alexander, explains that secrecy of the Constitutional Convention surprisingly was not even criticized by the members of the press at the time.

The response to the delegates' decision to wrap their activities in secrecy demonstrates how the media itself deferred to the convention. The [Pennsylvania] *Herald* broke the story on June 2 [1787] when it reported that the delegates found it difficult to communicate with one another because the convention was marked by such circumspection and secrecy. In fact, the concern for secrecy actually caused the delegates to suspend debate if one of their "inferior officers" entered the room. Considering that the convention was indeed news and that the press

public mind would be startled with propositions of royalty. The quondam [former] Tories have undoubtedly conceived hopes of a future union with Great Britain, from the inefficacy of our government and the tumults which prevailed in Massachusetts during the last winter. I saw a letter written, at that period, by a clergyman of considerable reputation in Nova Scotia to a person of eminence in this state; stating the impossibility of our being happy under our present Constitution and proposing (now we could think and argue calmly on all the consequences) that the efforts of the moderate, the virtuous and the brave should be exerted to effect a reunion with the parent state. He mentioned among other things, how instrumental the Cincinnati[1] might be and how much it would

---

1. The Cincinnati was a group founded by army officers who served together during the Revolutionary War. The group's name refers to Cincinnatus, a Roman emperor and was an allusion to the return of officers to civilian pursuits. George Washington was its first president.

---

thrived on filling space with political material, one might expect publishers to have questioned the secrecy rule. That was not the case. [The Herald editor Alexander] Dallas said the secrecy rule would naturally increase the people's anxiety, but he did not contend the proceedings should become public. He merely called for dispatch in remedying the Union's problems. Twenty-six other publishers reprinted this commentary. Thomas Greenleaf, editor of one of the few newspapers that adopted an Antifederalist position once the Constitution appeared, came the closest to suggesting the convention's deliberations should be made public. And Greenleaf merely promised that "no pains shall be spared to procure the debates and resolutions of the Convention for the inspection of the public as soon as any of them transpire." His pronouncement offered in the June 7 *New York Journal* hardly constituted an attack on the right of the delegates to conduct their affairs in secret.

John K. Alexander, *The Selling of the Constitutional Convention: A History of News Coverage.* Madison, WI: Madison House Press, 1990, p. 63.

redound to their emolument [salaries]. It seems by a conversation I have had here, that the ultimate practicability of introducing the Bishop of Osnaburgh is not a novel idea among those who were formerly termed Loyalists.[2] Ever since the peace, it has been occasionally talked of and wished for. Yesterday, where I dined, half [in] jest, and half [in] earnest, he [King George III's son, Frederick] was given as the first toast.

A Dangerous Time for Rumors

I leave you now, my dear friend, to reflect how ripe we are for the most mad and ruinous projects that can be suggested, especially when, in addition to this view, we take into consideration how thoroughly the patriotic part of the community, the friends of an efficient government are discouraged with the present system and irritated at the popular demagogues who are determined to keep themselves in office at the risque of every thing. Thence apprehensions are formed, that though the measures proposed by the convention may not be equal to the wishes of the most enlightened and virtuous, yet that they will be too high-toned to be adopted by our popular assemblies. Should that happen our political ship will be left afloat on a sea of chance, without a rudder as well as without a pilot.

I am happy to see you have had the honest boldness to attack in a public paper, the antifederal dogmas of a great personage in your State [George Clinton, the Governor of New York]. Go on and prosper. Were the men of talents and honesty, throughout the continent, properly combined into one phalanx, I am confident they would be competent to hew their way through all opposition. Were there no little jealousies, bickerings, and unworthy sinister views to divert them from their object, they might by perseverance establish a government calculated to promote the happiness of mankind and to make the Revolution a blessing instead of a curse.

2. In his letter to Col. Wadsworth, Alexander Hamilton included a letter which he said was circulating in New York. The letter suggested that King George III's son, Frederick, the Duke of York and the secular Bishop of Osnaburgh, should be made King of the United States.

Wrapping-Up the Convention

Constitutional Convention Delegates

> After months of heated debate, the time came, on Monday, September 17, 1787, for the delegates to sign the U.S. Constitution before sending it to the Confederation Congress and the states for their approval. This excerpt, from the last minutes on the last day of the Constitutional Convention, illustrates the belief held by many delegates that unanimous support was necessary to encourage ratification by the states. In the end, while all state delegations approved the document, not all of the delegates agreed to sign. Delegates Elbridge Gerry of Massachusetts, and George Mason and Edmund Randolf of Virginia, although extremely active during the Convention, refused to sign the document despite Benjamin Franklin's pleas for unanimous support.

The engrossed Constitution being read, DR. [BENJAMIN] FRANKLIN rose with a speech in his hand, which he had reduced to writing for his own conveniency, and which Mr. [James] Wilson read in the words following:

MR. PRESIDENT

I confess that there are several parts of this constitution which I do not at present approve, but I am not sure I shall never approve them: For having lived long, I have experienced many instances of being obliged by better information, or fuller consideration, to change opinions even

Reprinted from *The Debates in the Federal Convention of 1787 Which Framed the Constitution of the United States of America,* reported by James Madison, international edition, edited by Gaillard Hunt and James Brown Scott (New York: Oxford University Press, 1920).

on important subjects, which I once thought right, but found to be otherwise. It is therefore that the older I grow, the more apt I am to doubt my own judgment, and to pay more respect to the judgment of others. Most men, indeed, as well as most sects in religion, think themselves in possession of all truth, and that wherever others differ from them it is so far error. Steele a Protestant in a dedication tells the Pope, that the only difference between our churches in their opinions of the certainty of their doctrines is, the Church of Rome is infallible and the Church of England is never in the wrong. But though many private persons think almost as highly of their own infallibility as of that of their sect, few express it so naturally as a certain French lady, who in a dispute with her sister, said "I don't know how it happens, Sister but I meet with no body but myself, that's always in the right."

I Expect No Better Constitution

In these sentiments, Sir, I agree to this constitution with all its faults, if they are such; because I think a general government necessary for us, and there is no form of government but what may be a blessing to the people if well administered, and believe farther that this is likely to be well administered for a course of years, and can only end in despotism, as other forms have done before it, when the people shall become so corrupted as to need despotic government, being incapable of any other. I doubt too whether any other convention we can obtain, may be able to make a better constitution. For when you assemble a number of men to have the advantage of their joint wisdom, you inevitably assemble with those men all their prejudices, their passions, their errors of opinion, their local interests and their selfish views. From such an assembly can a perfect production be expected? It therefore astonishes me, Sir, to find this system approaching so near to perfection as it does; and I think it will astonish our enemies, who are waiting with confidence to hear that our councils are confounded like those of the builders of Babel; and that our states are on the point of separation, only to meet hereafter for the purpose of cutting one another's throats. Thus I consent, Sir, to this constitution because I expect no better and because I am not sure that it is not the best. The opinions I have had of its errors, I sacrifice to the public good. I have never whispered a syllable of them abroad. Within these walls they were born, and here they shall die. If every one of us in returning to our constituents were to report the objections he has had to it, and endeavor to gain partizans in support of them, we might prevent its being generally received and thereby lose all the salutary effects and great advantages resulting naturally in our favor among foreign nations as well as among ourselves, from our real or apparent unanimity. Much of the strength and efficiency of any government in procuring and securing happiness to the people, depends, on opinion, on the general opinion of the goodness of the government, as well as of the wisdom and integrity of its governors. I hope therefore that for our own sakes as a part of the people, and for the sake of posterity, we shall act heartily and unanimously in recommending this constitution (if approved by Congress and confirmed by the [state] conventions) wherever our influence may extend, and turn our future thoughts and endeavors to the means of having it well administred.

On the whole, Sir, I can not help expressing a wish that every member of the Convention who may still have objections to it, would with me, on this occasion doubt a little of his own infallibility, and to make manifest our unanimity, put his name to this instrument.

He then moved that the Constitution be signed by the members and offered the following as a convenient form viz. "Done in Convention by the unanimous consent of *the States* present the 17th of September, etc.—In witness whereof we have hereunto subscribed our names.". . .

Refusing to Sign

On the question to agree to the Constitution enrolled in order to be signed. It was agreed to all the States answering ay.

MR. [EDMUND] RANDOLPH then rose and, with an allusion to the observations of Dr. Franklin, apologized for his

On Monday, September 17, 1787, all but three delegates agreed to sign the Constitution.

refusing to sign the Constitution notwithstanding the vast majority and venerable names that would give sanction to its wisdom and its worth. He said however that he did not mean by this refusal to decide that he should oppose the Constitution without doors. He meant only to keep himself free to be governed by his duty as it should be prescribed by his future judgment. He refused to sign because he thought the object of the Convention would be frustrated by the alternative which it presented to the people. Nine states will fail to ratify the plan and confusion must ensue. With such a view of the subject he ought not, he could not, by pledging himself to support the plan, restrain himself from taking such steps as might appear to him most consistent with the public good.

MR. [GOUVERNEUR] MORRIS said that he too had objections, but considering the present plan as the best that was to be attained, he should take it with all its faults. The majority had determined in its favor and by that determination he should abide. The moment this plan goes forth all other considerations will be laid aside, and the great question will be, shall there be a national government or not? This must take place, or a general anarchy will be the alternative. He remarked that the signing in the form proposed related only to the fact that the *states* present were unanimous.

MR. [HUGH] WILLIAMSON suggested that the signing should be confined to the letter accompanying the Constitution to Congress, which might perhaps do nearly as well, and would he found be satisfactory to some members who disliked the Constitution. For himself he did not think a better plan was to be expected and had no scruples against putting his name to it.

MR. [ALEXANDER] HAMILTON expressed his anxiety that every member should sign. A few characters of consequence, by opposing or even refusing to sign the Constitution, might do infinite mischief by kindling the latent sparks which lurk under an enthusiasm in favor of the Convention which may soon subside. No man's ideas were more remote from the plan than his were known to be, but is it possible to deliberate between anarchy and convulsion on one side, and the chance of good to be expected from the plan on the other.

MR. [WILLIAM] BLOUNT said he had declared that he would not sign, so as to pledge himself in support of the plan, but he was relieved by the form proposed and would without committing himself attest the fact that the plan was the unanimous act of the states in convention.

The Hope to Prevent Great Mischief

DR. FRANKLIN expressed his fears from what Mr. Randolph had said, that he thought himself alluded to in the remarks offered this morning to the House. He declared that when drawing up that paper he did not know that any particular member would refuse to sign his name to the instrument and hoped to be so understood. He professed a high sense of obligation to Mr. Randolph for having brought forward the plan in the first instance and for the assistance he had given in its progress, and hoped that he would yet lay aside his objections, and by concurring with this brethren, prevent the great mischief which the refusal of his name might produce.

MR. RANDOLPH could not but regard the signing in the proposed form, as the same with signing the Constitution. The change of form therefore could make no difference with him. He repeated that in refusing to sign the Constitution, he took a step which might be the most awful of his life, but it was dictated by his conscience, and it was not possible for him to hesitate, much less, to change. He repeated also his persuasion, that the holding out this plan with a final alternative to the people, of accepting or rejecting it in toto, would really produce the anarchy and civil convulsions which were apprehended from the refusal of individuals to sign it.

MR. [ELBRIDGE] GERRY described the painful feelings of his situation, and the embarrassment under which he rose to offer any further observations on the subject which had been finally decided. Whilst the plan was depending, he had treated it with all the freedom he thought it deserved. He now felt himself bound as he was disposed to treat it with the respect due to the Act of the Convention. He hoped he should not violate that respect in declaring on this occasion his fears that a civil war may result from the present crises of the U.S. In Massachusetts, particularly he saw the danger of this calamitous event. In that state there are two parties, one devoted to democracy, the worst he thought of all political evils, the other as violent in the opposite extreme. From the collision of these in opposing and resisting the Constitution, confusion was greatly to be feared. He had thought it necessary, for this and other reasons that the plan should have been proposed in a more mediating shape, in order to abate the heat and opposition of parties. As it has been passed by the Convention, he was persuaded it would have a contrary effect. He could not therefore by signing the Constitution pledge himself to abide by it at all events. The proposed form made no difference with him. But if it were not otherwise apparent, the refusals to sign should never be known from him. Alluding to the remarks of Dr. Franklin, he could not he said but view them as levelled at himself and the other gentlemen who meant not to sign.

GENERAL [CHARLES] PINCKNEY. We are not likely to gain many converts by the ambiguity of the proposed form of signing. He thought it best to be candid and let the form speak to the substance. If the meaning of the signers be left in doubt, his purpose would not be answered. He should sign the Constitution with a view to support it with all his influence, and wished to pledge himself accordingly.

DR. FRANKLIN. It is too soon to pledge ourselves before Congress and our constituents shall have approved the plan.

MR. [JARED] INGERSOL did not consider the signing, either as a mere attestation of the fact or as pledging the signers to support the Constitution at all events, but as a recommendation, of what, all things considered, was the most eligible. . . .

A Rising Sun

The members then proceeded to sign the instrument.

Whilst the last members were signing it Dr. Franklin looking towards the President's chair, at the back of which a rising sun happened to be painted, observed to a few members near him, that painters had found it difficult to distinguish in their art a rising from a setting sun. I have said he, often and often in the course of the session, and the vicisitudes of my hopes and fears as to its issue, looked at that behind the President without being able to tell whether it was rising or setting: But now at length I have the happiness to know that it is a rising and not a setting Sun.

The Constitution being signed by all the members except Mr. Randolph, Mr. Mason, and Mr. Gerry who declined giving it the sanction of their names, the Convention dissolved itself by an Adjournment.

Chapter 3

Major Debates in the Convention

HISTORY
FIRSTHAND

Chapter Preface

I n *Federalist No. 51,* one of eighty-five essays written to urge New York to ratify the Constitution, James Madison clearly describes the fundamental challenge in creating a system of government:

> If men were angels, no government would be necessary. If angels were to govern men, neither external nor internal controls on government would be necessary. In framing a government which is to be administered by men over men, the great difficulty is this: you must first establish government to control the governed; and in the next place oblige it to control itself.

The men at the Constitutional Convention had begun to believe that a government that is too weak, such as the one created by the Articles of Confederation, would lead to anarchy. Out of this anarchy some charismatic individual might come forward and become a dictator. On the other hand, the framers worried that if the Constitution granted too much authority to the government, then it would ignore the wishes of the citizens it was meant to protect and serve.

In addition to recognizing this dilemma, the convention delegates needed to design specific mechanisms whereby this delicate balancing act could be achieved. Out of the deliberations among the delegates emerged three related principles by which they hoped this fundamental dilemma of government could be solved. First, they instituted a separation of powers. The work to be done by the national government would be divided into three separate branches. The legislative branch would write the laws, the executive branch would implement the laws, and the judicial branch would interpret the laws. By dividing the power of the national government into three distinct branches, the framers hoped that no one branch would ever gain complete supremacy over the other two branches.

Related to this was a system of checks and balances. Although each of the three branches of government would have distinct roles to play, their jobs would overlap. For example, the legislative branch would primarily be responsible for writing the laws for the national government; however, the executive branch could veto any law passed by the legislature. Whereas the judicial branch would interpret the laws, the president and the Senate could influence who would be serving as judges because the president would nominate and the Senate, by majority vote, would confirm all judicial appointments. The framers hoped that this system of overlapping jobs would provide further insurance that no one branch would become too powerful because no branch would have monopoly control over any given governmental task.

The U.S. Constitution divides governmental power even further. The delegates created a federal system in which governmental power was shared between the national government and the individual state governments. Once again, the framers hoped that sharing power would allow the state governments to stop the national government from exerting too much authority.

By dividing government power in these three ways, the framers felt more confident in granting the national government a greater role than it had under the Articles of Confederation.

Popular Rule or Mob Rule?: The Role of Citizens in the New Government

Constitutional Convention Delegates

> While the system of government created in the U.S. Constitution was democratic for its time, it is important to remember that there exist several limitations on popular rule in the Constitution. Debates held in the convention on May 31, 1787, illustrate that many of the Founding Fathers did not trust democracy. Others, to varying degrees, believed that the direct election of at least some national officials was an essential component of a successful government. On a split vote (six states in favor, two states opposed, and two states divided), it was decided that the direct election of members of the House of Representatives would be allowed.

The third resolution "that the national legislature ought to consist of two branches" was agreed to without debate or dissent, except that of Pennsylvania, given probably from complaisance to Doctor Franklin, who was understood to be partial to a single House of Legislation.

The fourth resolution, first clause: "that the members of the first branch of the National Legislature ought to be elected by the people of the several States" being taken up,

Reprinted from *The Debates in the Federal Convention of 1787 Which Framed the Constitution of the United States of America,* reported by James Madison, international edition, edited by Gaillard Hunt and James Brown Scott (New York: Oxford University Press, 1920).

MR. [ROGER] SHERMAN opposed the election by the people, insisting that it ought to be by the state legislatures. The people, he said, immediately should have as little to do as may be about the government. They want information and are constantly liable to be misled.

MR. [ELBRIDGE] GERRY. The evils we experience flow from the excess of democracy. The people do not want virtue, but are the dupes of pretended patriots. In Massachusetts it had been fully confirmed by experience that they are daily misled into the most baneful measures and opinions by the false re-

An Economic Interpretation of the Constitution

Many look to the Constitutional Convention and observe contentious political debates among competing visions of government. In 1913, Columbia University historian, Charles Beard, controversially argued instead that the U.S. Constitution should be seen fundamentally as a document designed to protect the economic interests of the Framers of the U.S. Constitution and other wealthy Americans.

The requirements for an economic interpretation of the formation and adoption of the Constitution may be stated in a hypothetical proposition which, although it cannot be verified absolutely from ascertainable data, will at once illustrate the problem and furnish a guide to research and generalization.

It will be admitted without controversy that the Constitution was the creation of a certain number of men, and it was opposed by a certain number of men.

Suppose it could be shown from the classification of the men who supported and opposed the Constitution that there was no line of property division at all; that is, that men owning substantially the same amounts of the same kinds of property were equally divided on the matter of adoption or rejection—it would then become apparent that the Constitution had no ascertainable relation to economic groups or

ports circulated by designing men, and which no one on the spot can refute. One principal evil arises from the want of due provision for those employed in the administration of government. It would seem to be a maxim of democracy to starve the public servants. He mentioned the popular clamour in Massachusetts for the reduction of salaries and the attack made on that of the governor though secured by the spirit of the Constitution itself. He had, he said, been too republican heretofore. He was still, however, republican, but had been taught by experience the danger of the levilling spirit.

---

classes but was the product of some abstract causes remote from the chief business of life—gaining a livelihood.

Suppose, on the other hand, that substantially all of the merchants, money lenders, security holders, manufacturers, shippers, capitalists, and financiers and their professional associates are to be found on one side in support of the Constitution and that substantially all or the major portion of the opposition came from the non-slaveholding farmers and the debtors—would it not be pretty conclusively demonstrated that our fundamental law was not the product of an abstraction known as "the whole people," but of a group of economic interests which must have expected beneficial results from its adoption? Obviously all the facts here desired cannot be discovered, but the data . . . bear out the latter hypothesis, and thus a reasonable presumption in favor of the theory is created.

Of course, it may be shown . . . that the farmers and debtors who opposed the Constitution were, in fact, benefited by the general improvement which resulted from its adoption. Nevertheless, it does not follow that the vague thing known as "the advancement of general welfare" or some abstraction known as "justice" was the immediate, guiding purpose of the leaders. . . . The point is, that the direct, impelling motive in both cases was the economic advantages which the beneficiaries expected would accrue to themselves first, from their action.

Charles A. Beard, *An Economic Interpretation of the Constitution of the United States,* 2nd ed. New York: The Macmillan Company, 1941, pp. 16–8.

MR. [GEORGE] MASON, argued strongly for an election of the larger branch by the people. It was to be the grand depository of the democratic principle of the government. It was, so to speak, to be our House of Commons. It ought to know and sympathise with every part of the community; and ought, therefore, to be taken not only from different parts of the whole republic, but also from different districts of the larger members of it, which had in several instances particularly in Virginia, different interests and views arising from difference of produce, of habits, etc. He admitted that we had been too democratic but was afraid we should incautiously run into the opposite extreme. We ought to attend to the rights of every class of the people. He had often wondered at the indifference of the superior classes of society to this dictate of humanity and policy; considering that however affluent their circumstances or elevated their situations might be, the course of a few years, not only might, but certainly would, distribute their posterity throughout the lowest classes of society. Every selfish motive therefore, every family attachment, ought to recommend such a system of policy as would provide no less carefully for the rights and happiness of the lowest than of the highest orders of citizens.

MR. [JAMES] WILSON contended strenuously for drawing the most numerous branch of the legislature immediately from the people. He was for raising the federal pyramid to a considerable altitude and for that reason, wished to give it as broad a basis as possible. No government could long subsist without the confidence of the people. In a republican government this confidence was peculiarly essential. He also thought it wrong to increase the weight of the state legislatures by making them the electors of the national legislature. All interference between the general and local governments should be obviated as much as possible. On examination it would be found that the opposition of states to federal measures had proceded much more from the officers of the states than from the people at large.

MR. [JAMES] MADISON considered the popular election of one branch of the national legislature as essential to every plan of free government. He observed that in some of the states one branch of the legislature was composed of men already removed from the people by an intervening body of electors. That if the first branch of the general legislature should be elected by the state legislatures, the second branch elected by the first—the Executive by the second together with the first; and other appointments again made for subordinate purposes by the Executive, the people would be lost sight of altogether; and the necessary sympathy between them and their rulers and officers, too little felt. He was an advocate for the policy of refining the popular appointments by successive filtrations, but thought it might be pushed too far. He wished the expedient to be resorted to only in the appointment of the second branch of the legislature, and in the executive and judiciary branches of the government. He thought too that the great fabric to be raised would be more stable and durable, if it should rest on the solid foundation of the people themselves, than if it should stand merely on the pillars of the legislatures.

Mr. Gerry did not like the election by the people. The maxims taken from the British constitution were often fallacious when applied to our situation, which was extremely different. Experience, he said, had shown that the state legislatures drawn immediately from the people did not always possess their confidence. He had no objection however to an election by the people if it were so qualified that men of honor & character might not be unwilling to be joined in the appointments. He seemed to think the people might nominate a certain number out of which the state legislatures should be bound to choose.

MR. [PIERCE] BUTLER thought an election by the people an impracticable mode.

On the question for an election of the first branch of the national Legislature by the people,

Massachusetts aye. Connecticut divided. New York aye. New Jersey no. Pennsylvania aye. Delaware divided. Virginia aye. North Carolina aye. South Carolina no. Georgia aye.

Representation: Population or Equality of the States?

Constitutional Convention Delegates

A major question in the Constitutional Convention was whether the number of representatives to the legislature would be based on population or if it would be based on equal representation for each state regardless of population. The populous states, not surprisingly, preferred a system based on population. They supported the Virginia Plan that was proposed by Governor Edmund Randolph of Virginia. The Virginia Plan had a bicameral legislature, each house of which was to be apportioned based on the state's population. The small states preferred the New Jersey Plan, proposed by New Jersey delegate William Paterson. The New Jersey Plan proposed a single national legislature with equal representation for each state. The two plans—and the underlying tensions between the populous states and the small states—often led to some of the more contentious debates in the convention.

These debates from June 9, 11, and 12, 1787, illustrate how deeply divided the large and small states were. For that reason, adoption of a plan in which one house would be elected based on population (the House of Representatives) and one house would be elected based on equal representation for each state (the Senate) has come to be known as the Great Compromise.

Reprinted from *The Debates in the Federal Convention of 1787 Which Framed the Constitution of the United States of America,* reported by James Madison, international edition, edited by Gaillard Hunt and James Brown Scott (New York: Oxford University Press, 1920).

M R. [WILLIAM] PATERSON moves that the Committee resume the clause relating to the rule of suffrage in the national legislature.

MR. [DAVID] BREARLY seconds him. He was sorry he said that any question on this point was brought into view. It had been much agitated in Congress at the time of forming the Confederation, and was then rightly settled by allowing to each sovereign state an equal vote. Otherwise the smaller states must have been destroyed instead of being saved. The substitution of a ratio, he admitted carried fairness on the face of it, but on a deeper examination was unfair and unjust. Judging of the disparity of the states by the quota of Congress Virginia would have 16 votes, and Georgia but one. A like proportion to the others will make the whole number ninety. There will be 3 large states and 10 small ones. The large states by which he meant Massachusetts, Pennsylvania and Virginia will carry every thing before them. It had been admitted, and was known to him from facts within New Jersey that where large and small counties were united into a district for electing representatives for the district, the large counties always carried their point, and consequently that the large states would do so. Virginia with her sixteen votes will be as solid column indeed, a formidable phalanx. While Georgia with her solitary vote and the other little states will be obliged to throw themselves constantly into the scale of some large one in order to have any weight at all. He had come to the convention with a view of being as useful as he could in giving energy and stability to the federal government. When the proposition for destroying the equality of votes came forward, he was astonished; he was alarmed. Is it fair then it will be asked that Georgia should have an equal vote with Virginia? He would not say it was. What remedy then? One only, that a map of the United States be spread out, that all the existing boundaries be erased, and that a new partition of the whole be made into 13 equal parts.

MR. PATERSON considered the proposition for a proportional representation as striking at the existence of the lesser States. He would premise however to an investigation of this question some remarks on the nature structure and powers of the Convention. The Convention he said was formed in pursuance of an Act of Congress that this act was recited in several of the commissions, particularly that of Massachusetts which he required to be read: that the amendment of the confederacy was the object of all the laws and commissions on the subject; that the Articles of Confederation were therefore the proper basis of all the proceedings of the convention. We ought to keep within its limits, or we should be charged by our constituents with usurpation, that the people of America were sharpsighted and not to be deceived. But the commissions under which we acted were not only the measure of our power; they denoted also the sentiments of the states on the subject of our deliberation. The idea of a national government as contradistinguished from a federal one, never entered into the mind of any of them, and to the public mind we must accomodate ourselves. We have no power to go beyond the federal scheme, and if we had the people are not ripe for any other. We must follow the people; the people will not follow us. The *proposition* could not be maintained whether considered in reference to us as a nation, or as a confederacy. A confederacy supposes sovereignty in the members composing it, and sovereignty supposes equality. If we are to be considered as a nation, all state distinctions must be abolished, the whole must be thrown into hotchpot [hodge podge], and when an equal division is made, then there may be fairly an equality of representation. He held up Virginia, Massachusetts and Pennsylvania as the three large states, and the other ten as small ones; repeating the calculations of Mr. Brearly as to the disparity of votes which would take place, and affirming that the small states would never agree to it. He said there was no more reason that a great individual State contributing much should have more votes than a small one contributing little, than that a rich individual citizen should have more votes than an indigent one. If the rateable property of A was to that of B as 40 to 1, ought A for that reason to have 40 times as many votes as B? Such a principle would never be

As characterized in this cartoon, the delegates to the Constitutional Convention argued their convictions passionately during the heated debates.

admitted, and if it were admitted would put B entirely at the mercy of A. As A has more to be protected than B so he ought to contribute more for the common protection. The same may be said of a large State which has more to be protected than a small one. Give the large states an influence in proportion of their magnitude, and what will be the consequence? Their ambition will be proportionally increased, and the small States will have every thing to fear. It was once proposed . . . that America should be represented in the British Parliament and then be bound by its laws. America could not have been entitled to more than 1/3 of the number of representatives which would fall to the share of Great Britain. Would American rights & interests have been safe under an authority thus constituted? It has been said that if a national government is to be formed so as to operate on the people and not on the states, the representatives ought to be drawn from the people. But why so? May not a legislature filled by the state legislatures operate on the people who choose the state legislatures? Or may not a practicable coercion be found? He admitted that there was none such in the existing system. He was attached strongly to the plan of the existing confederacy, in which the people choose their legislative representatives; and the legislatures their federal representatives. No other amendments were wanting than to mark the orbits of the States with due precision, and provide for the use of coercion, which was the great point. He alluded to the hint thrown out heretofore by Mr. Wilson of the necessity to which the large states might be reduced of confederating among themselves, by a refusal of the others to concur. Let them unite if they please, but let them remember that they have no authority to compel the others to unite. New Jersey will never confederate on the plan before the committee. She would be swallowed up. He had rather submit to a monarch, to a despot, than to such a fate. He would not only oppose the plan here but on his return home do every thing in his power to defeat it there.

Equal Numbers of People Should Have Equal Numbers of Representatives

MR. [JAMES] WILSON hoped if the Confederacy should be dissolved, that a *majority,* that a *minority* of the States would unite for their safety. He entered elaborately into the defence of a proportional representation, stating for his first position that as all authority was derived from the people, equal numbers of people ought to have an equal number of representatives, and different numbers of people different numbers of representatives. This principle had been improperly violated in the Confederation, owing to the urgent circumstances of the time. As to the case of A and B, stated by Mr. Paterson, he observed that in districts as large as the states, the number of people was the best measure of their comparative wealth. Whether therefore wealth or numbers were to form the ratio it would be the same. Mr. Paterson admitted persons, not property to be the measure of suffrage. Are not the citizens of Pennsylvania equal to those of New Jersey? Does it require 150 of the former to balance 50 of the latter? Representatives of different districts ought clearly to hold the same proportion to each other, as their respective constituents hold to each other. If the small states will not confederate on this plan, Pennsylvania and he presumed some other states, would not confederate on any other. We have been told that each state being sovereign, all are equal. So each man is naturally a sovereign over himself, and all men are therefore naturally equal. Can he retain this equality when he becomes a member of civil government? He can not. As little can a sovereign state, when it becomes a member of a federal government. If New Jersey will not part with her sovereignty, it is in vain to talk of Government. A new partition of the states is desireable, but evidently and totally impracticable.

Mr. [HUGH] WILLIAMSON, illustrated the cases by a comparison of the different states, to counties of different sizes within the same state; observing that proportional representation was admitted to be just in the latter case, and could not therefore be fairly contested in the former.

The question being about to be put Mr. Patterson hoped that as so much depended on it, it might be thought best to postpone that decision till tomorrow, which was done.

The committee rose and the House adjourned.

Toward a Compromise

[Monday, June 11] The clause concerning the rule of suffrage in the national legislature postponed on Saturday as resumed.

Mr. [ROGER] SHERMAN proposed that the proportion of suffrage in the first branch should be according to the respective numbers of free inhabitants and that in the second branch or Senate, each state should have one vote and no more. He said as the states would remain possessed of certain individual rights, each state ought to be able to protect itself; otherwise a few large states will rule the rest. The House of Lords in England, he observed, had certain particular rights under the Constitution, and hence they have an equal vote with the House of Commons that they may be able to defend their rights.

Mr. [JOHN] RUTLIDGE proposed that the proportion of suffrage in the first branch should be according to the quotas of contribution. The justice of this rule he said could not be contested. Mr. [Pierce] Butler urged the same idea: adding that money was power; and that the states ought to have weight in the government in proportion to their wealth. . . .

Benjamin Franklin's Proposal

DR. [BENJAMIN] FRANKLIN said he had thrown his ideas of the matter on a paper which Mr. Wilson read to the Committee in the words following—

MR. CHAIRMAN

It has given me great pleasure to observe that till this point, the proportion of representation, came before us, our debates were carried on with great coolness and temper. If anything of a contrary kind, has on this occasion appeared, I hope it will not be repeated; for we are sent here to *consult,* not to *contend,* with each other; and declarations of a fixed opinion, and of determined resolution, never to change it, neither enlighten nor convince us. Positiveness and warmth on one side, naturally beget their like on the other and tend to create and augment discord and division in a great concern, wherein harmony and union are extremely necessary to give weight to our councils, and render them effectual in promoting and securing the common good.

I must own that I was originally of opinion it would be better if every member of Congress, or our national council, were to consider himself rather as a representative of the whole, than as an agent for the interests of a particular state; in which case the proportion of members for each state would be of less consequence, and it would not be very material whether they voted by states or individually. But as I find this is not to be expected, I now think the number of representatives should bear some proportion to the number of the represented and that the decisions should be by the majority of members, not by the majority of states. This is objected to from an apprehension that the greater states would then swallow up the smaller. I do not at present clearly see what advantage the greater states could propose to themselves by swallowing the smaller, and therefore do not apprehend they would attempt it. I recollect that in the beginning of this century, when the Union was proposed of the two Kingdoms, England & Scotland, the Scotch patriots were full of fears, that unless they had an equal number of representatives in Parliament, they should be ruined by the superiority of the English. They finally agreed, however, that the different proportions of importance in the Union of the two Nations should be attended to, whereby they [Scotland] were to have only forty members in the House of Commons, and only sixteen in the House of Lords. A very great inferiority of numbers! And yet to this day I do not recollect that anything has been done in the Parliament of Great Britain to the prejudice of Scotland, and whoever looks over the lists of public officers, civil & military of that nation will find I believe that the North Britons [the Scots] enjoy at least their full proportion of emolument [benefits]. . . .

The greater states, Sir, are naturally as unwilling to have their property left in the disposition of the smaller, as the smaller are to have theirs in the disposition of the greater. An honorable gentleman has, to avoid this difficulty, hinted a proposition of equalizing the states. It appears to me an equitable one, and I should, for my own part, not be against such a measure, if it might be found practicable. Formerly, indeed, when almost every province had a different constitution, some with greater others with fewer privileges, it was of importance to the borderers when their boundaries were contested, whether by running the division lines, they were placed on one side or the other. At present when such differences are done away, it is less material. The interest of a state is made up of the interests of its individual members. If they are not injured, the state is not injured. Small states are more easily well and happily governed than large ones. If therefore in such an equal division, it should be found necessary to diminish Pennsylvania, I should not be averse to the giving a part of it to New Jersey, and another to Delaware. But as there would probably be considerable difficulties in adjusting such a division; and however equally made at first, it would be continually varying by the augmentation of inhabitants in some States, and their fixed proportion in others; and thence frequent occasion for new divisions, I beg leave to propose for the consideration of the Committee another mode, which appears to me, to be as equitable, more easily carried into practice, and more permanent in its nature.

Let the weakest State say what proportion of money or force it is able and willing to furnish for the general purposes of the Union.

Let all the others oblige themselves to furnish each an equal proportion.

The whole of these joint supplies to be absolutely in the disposition of Congress.

The Congress in this case to be composed of an equal number of delegates from each state.

And their decisions to be by the majority of individual members voting.

If these joint and equal supplies should on particular occasions not be sufficient, let Congress make requisitions on the richer and more powerful states for farther aids, to be voluntarily afforded, leaving to each state the right of considering the necessity and utility of the aid desired, and of giving more or less as it should be found proper.

This mode is not new; it was formerly practised with success by the British government with respect to Ireland and the Colonies. We sometimes gave even more than they expected or thought just to accept; and in the last war carried on while we were united, they gave us back in 5 years a million Sterling. We should probably have continued such voluntary contributions, whenever the occasions appeared to require them for the common good of the Empire. It was not till they chose to force us and to deprive us of the merit and pleasure of voluntary contributions that we refused and resisted. Those contributions however were to be disposed of at the pleasure of a government in which we had no representative. I am therefore persuaded, that they will not be refused to one in which the representation shall be equal.

The President: Creating an American King?

Constitutional Convention Delegates

> Given the history of the United States (especially the bitter
> war the Americans just fought in order to gain independence
> from the British king), many framers were concerned that
> consolidating the executive branch into one person would be
> a recipe for the creation of an American king. Some particu-
> larly feared the process of electing the president because,
> once in office, the president could use his power to insure his
> reelection. Benjamin Franklin shows concern that providing
> the president with a salary would attract the wrong type of
> people to the job and could speed the creation of an American
> king. For these reasons, the ability to impeach the president
> was considered an essential check on presidential power.

The Committee of the whole proceeded to the seventh
resolution, "that a national executive be instituted, to
be chosen by the national legislature—for the term of
years, etc., to be ineligible thereafter, to posses the executive powers of Congress, etc."

MR. [CHARLES] PINKNEY was for a vigorous executive but
was afraid the executive powers of the existing Congress might
extend to peace and war, etc., which would render the executive a monarchy of the worst kind, to wit an elective one.

Reprinted from *The Debates in the Federal Convention of 1787 Which Framed the Constitution of the United States of America,* reported by James Madison, international edition, edited by Gaillard Hunt and James Brown Scott (New York: Oxford University
Press, 1920).

MR. [JAMES] WILSON moved that the executive consist of a single person.

MR. PINKNEY seconded the motion, so as to read "that a national executive to consist of a single person be instituted."

A considerable pause ensuing and the Chairman asking if he should put the question, Dr. [Benjamin] Franklin observed that it was a point of great importance and wished that the gentlemen would deliver their sentiments on it before the question was put.

Opening Opinions

MR. [JOHN] RUTLEDGE animadverted [commented adversely] on the shyness of gentlemen on this and other subjects. He said it looked as if they supposed themselves precluded by having frankly disclosed their opinions from afterwards changing them, which he did not take to be at all the case. He said he was for vesting the executive power in a single person, though he was not for giving him the power of war and peace. A single man would feel the greatest responsibility and administer the public affairs best.

MR. [ROGER] SHERMAN said he considered the executive magistracy as nothing more than an institution for carrying the will of the legislature into effect, that the person or persons ought to be appointed by and accountable to the legislature only, which was the depositary of the supreme will of the society. As they were the best judges of the business which ought to be done by the executive department, and consequently of the number necessary from time to time for doing it, he wished the number might not be fixed, but that the legislature should be at liberty to appoint one or more as experience might dictate.

MR. WILSON preferred a single magistrate, as giving most energy dispatch and responsibility to the office. He did not consider the prerogatives of the British monarch as a proper guide in defining the executive powers. Some of these prerogatives were of a legislative nature. Among others that of war and peace etc. The only powers he conceived strictly executive were those of executing the laws, and appointing officers, not appertaining to and appointed by the legislature.

MR. [ELBRIDGE] GERRY favored the policy of annexing a council to the executive in order to give weight and inspire confidence.

MR. [EDMUND] RANDOLPH strenuously opposed a unity in the executive magistracy. He regarded it as the fetus of monarchy. We had, he said, no motive to be governed by the British government as our prototype. He did not mean however to throw censure on that excellent fabric. If we were in a situation to copy it he did not know that he should be opposed to it, but the fixed genius of the people of America required a different form of government. He could not see why the great requisites for the executive department, vigor, despatch and responsibility could not be found in three men as well as in one man. The executive ought to be independent. It ought therefore in order to support its independence to consist of more than one.

MR. WILSON said that unity in the executive instead of being the fetus of monarchy would be the best safeguard against tyranny. He repeated that he was not governed by the British model which was inapplicable to the situation of this country; the extent of which was so great, and the manners so republican, that nothing but a great confederated republic would do for it.

Mr. Wilson's motion for a single magistrate was postponed by common consent; the Committee seeming unprepared for any decision on it. . . .

Benjamin Franklin Worries About a Salaried President

[Saturday, June 2] DR. FRANKLIN moved that what related to the compensation for the services of the executive be postponed, in order to substitute—"whose necessary expences shall be defrayed, but who shall receive no salary, stipend fee or reward whatsoever for their services." He said that being very sensible of the effect of age on his memory, he had been unwilling to trust to that for the observations which seemed to support his motion, and had reduced them to writing, that he might with the permission of the Committee read instead of speaking them. Mr. Wilson made an offer to read the paper, which was accepted:

Sir.

It is with reluctance that I rise to express a disapprobation of any one article of the plan for which we are so much obliged to the honorable gentleman who laid it before us. From its first reading I have borne a good will to it, and in general wished it success. In this particular of salaries to the executive branch I happen to differ; and as my opinion may appear new and chimerical, it is only from a persuasion that it is right, and from a sense of duty that I hazard it. The Committee will judge of my reasons when they have heard them, and their judgment may possibly change mine. I think I see inconveniences in the appointment of salaries; I see none in refusing them, but on the contrary, great advantages.

Sir, there are two passions which have a powerful influence on the affairs of men. These are ambition and avarice; the love of power, and the love of money. Separately each of these has great force in prompting men to action; but when united in view of the same object, they have in many minds the most violent effects. Place before the eyes of such men, a post of *honor* that shall be at the same time a place of *profit,* and they will move heaven and earth to obtain it. The vast number of such places it is that renders the British government so tempestuous. The struggles for them are the true sources of all those factions which are perpetually dividing the nation, distracting its councils, hurrying sometimes into fruitless and mischievous wars, and often compelling a submission to dishonorable terms of peace.

And of what kind are the men that will strive for this profitable pre-eminence, through all the bustle of cabal [intrigue], the heat of contention, the infinite mutual abuse of parties, tearing to pieces the best of characters? It will not be the wise and moderate; the lovers of peace and good order, the men fittest for the trust. It will be the bold and the violent, the men of strong passions and indefatigable activity in their selfish pursuits. These will thrust themselves into your government and be your rulers. And these too will be mistaken in the expected happiness of their situation. For their vanquished competitors of the same spirit, and from the same motives will perpetually be endeavouring to distress their administration, thwart their measures and render them odious to the people.

Besides these evils, Sir, though we may sit out in the beginning with moderate salaries, we shall find that such will not be of long continuance. Reasons will never be wanting for proposed augmentations. And there will always be a party for giving more to the rulers, that the rulers may be able in return to give more to them. Hence as all history informs us, there has been in every state and kingdom a constant kind of warfare between the governing and governed. The one striving to obtain more for its support, and the other to pay less. And this has alone occasioned great convulsions, actual civil wars, ending either in dethroning of the princes or enslaving of the people. Generally indeed the ruling power carries its point; the revenues of princes constantly increasing, and we see that they are never satisfied, but always in want of more. The more the people are discontented with the oppression of taxes, the greater need the prince has of money to distribute among his partisans and pay the troops that are to suppress all resistance and enable him to plunder at pleasure. There is scarce a king in a hundred who would not, if he could, follow the example of Pharaoh, get first all the peoples money, then all their lands, and then make them and their children servants for ever. It will be said, that we don't propose to establish kings. I know it. But there is a natural inclination in mankind to kingly government. It sometimes relieves them from aristocratic domination. They had rather have one tyrant then five hundred. It gives more of the appearance of equality among citizens and that they like. I am apprehensive therefore, perhaps too apprehensive, that the government of these states may in future times end in a monarchy. But this catastrophe I think may be long delayed if in our proposed system we do not sow the seeds of contention, faction and tumult, by making our posts of honor, places of profit. If we do, I fear that though we do employ at first a number, and not a single person, the number will in time be set aside, it will only nourish the fetus of a king, as the honorable gentleman from Virginia [Edmund Randolph] very aptly expressed it, and a King will the sooner be set over us.

It may be imagined by some that this is an utopian idea, and that we can never find men to serve us in the executive department, without paying them well for their services. I conceive this to be a mistake. Some existing facts present themselves to me, which incline me to a contrary opinion. . . .

Have we not seen, the great and most important of our offices, that of General of our armies executed for eight years together without the smallest salary, by a patriot whom I will not now offend by any other praise [i.e., George Washington] and this through fatigues and distresses in common with the other brave men his military friends and companions, and the constant anxieties peculiar to his station? And shall we doubt finding three or four men in all the United States, with public spirit enough to bear sitting in peaceful council for perhaps an equal term, merely to preside over our civil concerns and see that our laws are duly executed. Sir, I have a better opinion of our country. I think we shall never be without a sufficient number of wise and good men to undertake and execute well and faithfully the office in question.

Sir, the saving of the salaries that may at first be proposed is not an object with me. The subsequent mischiefs of proposing them are what I apprehend. And, therefore, it is that I move the amendment. If it is not seconded or accepted I must be contented with the satisfaction of having delivered my opinion frankly and done my duty.

The motion was seconded by Col. Hamilton with the view he said merely of bringing so respectable a proposition before the Committee, and which was besides enforced by arguments that had a certain degree of weight. No debate ensued, and the proposition was postponed for the consideration of the members. It was treated with great respect, but rather for the author of it, than from any apparent conviction of its expediency or practicability.

Impeachment of the President

MR.[JOHN] DICKINSON moved "that the executive be made removeable by the national legislature on the request of a majority of the legislatures of individual states." It was necessary he said to place the power of removing somewhere. He did not like the plan of impeaching the great officers of state. He did not know how provision could be made for removal of them in a better mode than that which he had proposed. He had no idea of abolishing the state governments as some gentlemen seemed inclined to do. The happiness of this country in his opinion required considerable powers to be left in the hands of the states.

MR. BEDFORD seconded the motion.

MR. SHERMAN contended that the national legislature should have power to remove the executive at pleasure.

MR. MASON. Some mode of displacing an unfit magistrate is rendered indispensable by the fallibility of those who choose, as well as by the corruptibility of the man chosen. He opposed decidedly the making the executive the mere creature of the legislature as a violation of the fundamental principle of good government.

MR. MADISON & MR. WILSON observed that it would leave an equality of agency in the small with the great states; that it would enable a minority of the people to prevent the removal of an officer who had rendered himself justly criminal in the eyes of the majority; that it would open a door for intrigues against him in states where his administration thought just might be unpopular, and might tempt him to pay court to particular states whose leading partisans he might fear, or wish to engage as his partisans. They both thought it bad policy to introduce such a mixture of the state authorities, where their agency could be otherwise supplied.

MR. DICKINSON considered the business as so important that no man ought to be silent or reserved. He went into a discourse of some length, the sum of which was, that the legislative, executive and judiciary departments ought to be made as independent as possible; but that such an executive as some seemed to have in contemplation was not consistent with a republic: that a firm executive could only exist in a limited monarchy. In the British government itself the weight of the executive arises from the attachments which the Crown draws to itself, and not merely from the force of its prerogatives. In place of these attachments we must look out for something else. One source of stability is the double branch of the legislature. The division of the country into distinct states formed the other principal source of stability. This division ought therefore to be maintained, and considerable powers to be left with the states. This was the ground of his consolation for the future fate of his country. Without this, and in case of a consolidation of the states into one great republic, we might read its fate in the history of smaller ones. A limited monarchy he considered as *one* of the best governments in the world. It was not *certain* that the same blessings were derivable from any other form. It was certain that equal blessing had never yet been derived from any of the republican form. A limited monarchy however was out of the question. The spirit of the times—the state of our affairs—forbade the experiment, if it were desireable. Was it possible moreover in the nature of things to introduce it even if these obstacles were less insuperable? A House of Nobles was essential to such a government. Could these be created by a breath or by a stroke of the pen? No. They were the growth of ages and could only arise under a complication of circumstances none of which existed in this country. But though a form the most perfect *perhaps* in itself be unattainable, we must not despair. If ancient republics have been found to flourish for a moment only and then vanish for ever, it only proves that they were badly constituted; and that we ought to seek for every remedy for their diseases. One of these remedies he conceived to be the accidental lucky division of this country into distinct states, a division which some seemed desirous to abolish altogether. As to the point of representation in the national legislature as it might affect states of different sizes, he said it must probably end in mutual concession. He hoped that each state would retain an equal voice at least in one branch of the national legislature and supposed the sums paid within each state would form a better ratio for the other branch than either the number of inhabitants or the quantum of property.

A motion being made to strike out "on request by a majority of the legislatures of the individual states" and rejected, Connecticut, South Carolina & Georgia being aye, the rest no: the question was taken—

On Mr. Dickinson's motion for making the executive removeable by the national legislature at the request of a majority of State Legislatures which was also rejected —all the states being in the negative except Delaware which gave an affirmative vote.

President or Presidents?

MR. RUTLEDGE & MR. C. PINKNEY moved that the blank for the number of persons in the executive be filled with the words "one person." He supposed the reasons to be so obvious and conclusive in favor of one that no member would oppose the motion.

MR. RANDOLPH opposed it with great earnestness, declaring that he should not do justice to the country which sent him if he were silently to suffer the establishment of a unity in the executive department. He felt an opposition to it which he believed he should continue to feel as long as he lived. He urged first, that the permanent temper of the people was adverse to the very semblance of monarchy. Second, that a unity was unnecessary a plurality being equally competent to all the objects of the department. Third, that the necessary confidence would never be reposed in a single Magistrate. Fourth, that the appointments would generally be in favor of some inhabitant near the center of the community, and consequently the remote parts would not be on an equal footing. He was in favor of three members of the executive to be drawn from different portions of the country.

MR. [PIERCE] BUTLER contended strongly for a single magistrate as most likely to answer the purpose of the remote parts. If one man should be appointed he would be responsible to the whole, and would be impartial to its interests. If three or more should be taken from as many districts, there would a constant struggle for local advantages. In military matters this would be particularly mischievous. He said his opinion on this point had been formed under the opportunity he had had of seeing the manner in which a plurality of military heads distracted Holland when threatened with invasion by the imperial troops. One man was for directing the force to the defence of this part, another to that part of the country, just as he happened to be swayed by prejudice or interest.

[Monday, June 4] The question was resumed on motion "shall the blank for the number of the Executive be filled with a single person?"

MR. WILSON was in favor of the motion. It had been opposed by the gentleman from Virginia [Mr. Randolph] but the arguments used had not convinced him. He observed that the objections of Mr. Randolph were levelled not so much against the measure itself, as against its unpopularity. If he could suppose that it would occasion a rejection of the plan of which it should form a part, though the part was an important one, yet he would give it up rather than lose the whole. On examination he could see no evidence of the alledged antipathy of the people. On the contrary he was persuaded that it does not exist. All know that a single magistrate is not a king. One fact has great weight with him. All the 13 states though agreeing in scarce any other instance, agree in placing a single magistrate at the head of the government. The idea of three heads has taken place in none. The degree of power is indeed different, but there are no coordinate heads. In addition to his former reasons for preferring a unity, he would mention another. The *tranquility* not less than the vigor of the government he thought would be favored by it. Among three equal members, he foresaw nothing but uncontrolled, continued, & violent animosities; which would not only interrupt the public administration; but diffuse their poison through the other branches of government, through the states, and at length through the people at large. If the members were to be unequal in power the principle of the opposition to the unity was given up. If equal, the making them an odd number would not be a remedy. In courts of justice there are two sides only to a question. In the legislative and executive departments questions have commonly many sides. Each member therefore might espouse a separate one and no two agree.

MR. SHERMAN. This matter is of great importance and ought to be well considered before it is determined. Mr. Wilson he said had observed that in each state a single magistrate was placed at the head of the government. It was so he admitted, and properly so, and he wished the same policy to prevail in the federal government. But then it should be also remarked that in all the states there was a council of advice, without which the first magistrate could not act. A council he thought necessary to make the establishment acceptable to the people. Even in Great Britain the King has a council; and though he appoints it himself, its advice has its weight with him, and attracts the confidence of the people.

MR. WILLIAMSON asks Mr. Wilson whether he means to annex a council.

MR. WILSON means to have no council, which oftener serves to cover, than prevent malpractices.

MR. GERRY was at a loss to discover the policy of three members for the executive. It would be extremely inconvenient in many instances, particularly in military matters, whether relating to the militia, an army or a navy. It would be a general with three heads.

On the question for a single Executive it was agreed to Massachusetts aye. Connecticut aye. New York no. Pennsylvania aye. Delaware no. Maryland no. Virginia aye. North Carolina aye. South Carolina aye. Georgia aye.

Slavery and
the Slave Trade

Constitutional Convention Delegates

Long before the Constitutional Convention, slavery was a
divisive issue in America. By 1787, Pennsylvania, Massachusetts, Connecticut, Rhode Island, New York, and New Jersey
had all abolished slavery. Some states, especially Maryland
and Virginia, were willing to stop the importation of new
slaves but did not want to abolish slavery altogether. Other
states, especially Georgia and South Carolina, refused to prohibit either slavery or the slave trade. With such an array of
opinions and beliefs, slavery threatened to play a blocking
role in the debate over the Constitution.

As the selection of debates concerning slavery excerpted
here suggests, slavery mattered most of all in terms of taxation and representation. The southern states wanted slaves to
be counted in determining population (which was the basis of
the number of seats each state would get in the House of Representatives) but not in terms of taxation. The northern states
feared that this arrangement would allow the southern states
to have an unnaturally large number of representatives in the
House while avoiding their share of taxes. The solution,
known as the Three-Fifths Compromise, established that in
terms of population and taxation only, slaves would count as
three-fifths of a person. It did *not* grant slaves three-fifths of
the rights or liberties enjoyed by other Americans.

Surprisingly, the debate over the slave trade was not as
prominent as some had hoped and others had feared. Some

Reprinted from *The Debates in the Federal Convention of 1787 Which Framed the Constitution of the United States of America,* reported by James Madison, international edition, edited by Gaillard Hunt and James Brown Scott (New York: Oxford University
Press, 1920).

of this is due to the fact that the debates over the slave trade were not held until late in the convention (August 8, 21, and 22, 1787). By that time, many of the delegates were tired and were willing to make politically-expedient deals in order to return home to their families. Added to this, the delegates from South Carolina and Georgia made it clear that they would be unwilling to sign any document that abolished the slave trade. The eventual compromise that was reached was that the slave trade would not be abolished for at least twenty years.

M R. [PIERCE] BUTLER and GENERAL [CHARLES] PINKNEY insisted that blacks be included in the rule of representation, *equally* with the whites and for that purpose moved that the words "three-fifths" be struck out.

MR. [ELBRIDGE] GERRY thought that three-fifths of them was, to say the least, the full proportion that could be admitted.

MR. [NATHANIEL] GHORUM. This ratio was fixed by Congress as a rule of taxation. Then it was urged by the delegates representing the states having slaves that the blacks were still more inferior to freemen. At present when the ratio of representation is to be established, we are assured that they are equal to freemen. The arguments on a former occasion had convinced him that three-fifths was pretty near the just proportion and he should vote according to the same opinion now.

MR. BUTLER insisted that the labour of a slave in S. Carolina was as productive and valuable as that of a freeman in Massachusetts, that as wealth was the great means of defence and utility to the nation they were equally valuable to it with freemen and that, consequently, an equal representation ought to be allowed for them in a Government which was instituted principally for the protection of property and was itself to be supported by property.

MR. [GEORGE] MASON, could not agree to the motion, notwithstand it was favorable to Virginia because he thought it unjust. I was certain that the slaves were valuable, as they raised the value of land, increased the exports & imports, and of course the revenue, would supply the means of feeding & supporting an army, and might in cases of emergency become themselves soldiers. As in these important respects they were useful to the community at large, they ought not to be excluded from the estimate of representation. He could not however regard them as equal to freemen and could not vote for them as such. He added as worthy of remark, that the southern states have this peculiar species of property, over and above the other species of property common to all the States.

MR. [HUGH] WILLIAMSON reminded Mr. Ghorum that if the Southern states contended for the inferiority of blacks to whites when taxation was in view, the eastern states on the same occasion contended for their equality. He did not however either then or now, concur in either extreme, but approved of the ratio of three-fifths. . . .

The Most Grating Circumstance

[Wednesday, August 8, 1887] MR. [RUFUS] KING: The admission of slaves was a most grating circumstance to his mind, & he believed would be so to a great part of the people of America. He had not made a strenuous opposition to it heretofore because he had hoped that this concession would have produced a readiness which had not been manifested, to strengthen the general government and to mark a full confidence in it. The report under consideration had, by the tenor of it, put an end to all those hopes. In two great points the hands of the legislature were absolutely tied. The importation of slaves could not be prohibited—exports could not be taxed. Is this reasonable? What are the great objects of the general system? 1. defence against foreign invasion. 2. against internal sedition. Shall all the states then be bound to defend each, and shall each be at liberty to introduce a weakness which will render defense more difficult? Shall one part of the United States be bound to defend another part and that other part be at liberty not only to increase its own danger, but to withhold the compensation for the burden? If slaves are to be imported, shall not the exports produced by their labor, supply a revenue the better to enable the general government to defend their masters? There was so much inequality and unreasonableness in all this that the people of the northern states could never be reconciled to it. No candid man could undertake to justify it to them. He had hoped that some accomodation would have taken place on this subject; that at least a time would have been limited for the importation of slaves. He never could agree to let them be imported without limitation and then be represented in the national legislature. Indeed, he could so little persuade himself of the rectitude of such a practice that he was not sure he could assent to it under any circumstances. At all events, either slaves should not be represented, or exports should be taxable.

MR. [ROGER] SHERMAN regarded the slave trade as iniquitous; but the point of representation having been settled after much difficulty and deliberation, he did not think himself bound to make opposition, especially as the present article as amended did not preclude any arrangement whatever on that point in another place of the report.

MR. [JAMES] MADISON objected to 1 [representative] for every 40,000 inhabitants as a perpetual rule. The future increase of population if the Union should be permanent, will render the number of Representatives excessive.

MR. GHORUM. It is not to be supposed that the government will last so long as to produce this effect. Can it be supposed that this vast country including the western territory will 150 years hence remain one nation?

MR. [OLIVER] ELLSWORTH. If the government should continue so long, alterations may be made in the Constitution in the manner proposed in a subsequent article.

MR. SHERMAN AND MR. MADISON moved to insert the words "not exceeding" before the words "1 for every 40,000," which was agreed to.

Make All Men Citizens

MR. [GOUVERNEUR] MORRIS moved to insert "free" before the word, "inhabitants." Much he said would depend on this point. He never would concur in upholding domestic slavery.

It was a nefarious institution. It was the curse of heaven on the states where it prevailed. Compare the free regions of the Middle States, where a rich and noble cultivation marks the prosperity and happiness of the people, with the misery and poverty which overspread the barren wastes of Virginia Maryland and the other states having slaves. Travel through the whole continent and you behold the prospect continually varying with the appearance and disappearance of slavery. The moment you leave the Eastern states and enter New York, the effects of the institution become visible, passing through the Jerseys and entering Pennsylvania every criterion of superior improvement witnesses the change. Proceed southwardly and every step you take through the great region of slaves presents a desert increasing, with the increasing proportion of these wretched beings. Upon what principle is it that the slaves shall be computed in the representation? Are they men? Then make them citizens and let them vote. Are they property? Why then is no other property included? The houses in this city [Philadelphia] are worth more than all the wretched slaves which cover the rice swamps of South Carolina. The admission of slaves into the representation when fairly explained comes to this: that the inhabitant of Georgia and South Carolina which goes to the Coast of Africa and, in defiance of the most sacred laws of humanity, tears away his fellow creatures from their dearest connections and damns them to the most cruel bondages, shall have more votes in a government instituted for protection of the rights of mankind than the citizen of Pennsylvania or New Jersey who views with a laudable horror, so nefarious a practice. He would add that domestic slavery is the most prominent feature in the aristocratic countenance of the proposed Constitution. The vassalage of the poor has ever been the favorite offspring of aristocracy. And what is the proposed compensation to the northern states for a sacrifice of every principle of right, of every impulse of humanity? They are to bind themselves to march their militia for the defence of the Southern states; for their defence against those very slaves of whom they complain. They must supply vessels & seamen in case of foreign attack. The legislature will have indefinite power to tax them by excises and duties on imports—both of which will fall heavier on them than on the southern inhabitants, for the tea used by a northern freeman will pay more tax than the whole consumption of the miserable slave, which consists of nothing more than his physical subsistence and the rag that covers his nakedness. On the other side the southern states are not to be restrained from importing fresh supplies of wretched Africans, at once to increase the danger of attack, and the difficulty of defence; nay, they are to be encouraged to it by an assurance of having their votes in the national government increased in proportion, and are at the same time to have their exports and their slaves exempt from all contributions for the public service. Let it not be said that direct taxation is to be proportioned to representation. It is idle to suppose that the general government can stretch its hand directly into the pockets of the people scattered over so vast a country. They can only do it through the medium of exports imports and excises. For what, then, are all these sacrifices to be made? He would sooner submit himself to a tax for paying for all the negroes in the United States than saddle posterity with such a Constitution. . . .

MR. SHERMAN. did not regard the admission of the negroes into the ratio of representation as liable to such insuperable objections. It was the freemen of the southern states who were in fact to be represented according to the taxes paid by them, and the negroes are only included in the estimate of the taxes. This was his idea of the matter.

MR. [CHARLES] PINKNEY, considered the fisheries and the western frontier as more burdensome to the United States than the slaves. He thought this could be demonstrated if the occasion were a proper one. . . .

Debate over Continuing the Import of Slaves

[Tuesday, August 21, 1787] MR. [LUTHER] MARTIN proposed to vary the Sect: 4. art VII. so as to allow a prohibition or tax on the importation of slaves. First, as five slaves are to be counted as three free men in the apportionment of Representatives, such a clause would leave an encouragement to this traffic. Second, slaves weakened one part of the Union which the other parts were bound to protect; the privilege of importing them was therefore unreasonable. Third, it was inconsistent with the principles of the revolution and dishonorable to the American character to have such a feature in the Constitution.

MR. [JOHN] RUTLEDGE did not see how the importation of slaves could be encouraged by this Section. He was not apprehensive of insurrections and would readily exempt the other states from the obligation to protect the southern against them. Religion and humanity had nothing to do with this question. Interest alone is the governing principle with nations. The true question at present is whether the southern states shall or shall not be parties to the Union. If the northern states consult their interest, they will not oppose the increase of slaves which will increase the commodities of which they will become the carriers.

MR. ELLSWORTH was for leaving the clause as it stands. Let every state import what it pleases. The morality or wisdom of slavery are considerations belonging to the states themselves. What enriches a part enriches the whole, and the States are the best judges of their particular interest. The old confederation had not meddled with this point, and he did not see any greater necessity for bringing it within the policy of the new one.

MR. [CHARLES] PINKNEY. South Carolina can never receive the plan if it prohibits the slave trade. In every proposed extension of the powers of the Congress, that state has expressly and watchfully excepted that of meddling with the importation of negroes. If the states be all left at liberty on this subject, South Carolina may perhaps by degrees do of herself what is wished, as Virginia and Maryland have already done. . . .

A National Sin

[Wednesday, August 22, 1787] MR. [ROGER] SHERMAN was for leaving the clause as it stands. He disapproved of the slave trade; yet as the states were now possessed of the right to import slaves, as the public good did not require it to be taken from them and as it was expedient to have as few objections as possible to the proposed scheme of government, he thought it best to leave the matter as we find it. He observed that the abolition of slavery seemed to be going on in the United States and that the good sense of the several states would probably by degrees complete it. He urged on the convention the necessity of despatching its business.

COL. MASON. This infernal traffic originated in the avarice of British merchants. The British government constantly checked the attempts of Virginia to put a stop to it. The present question concerns not the importing states alone but the whole Union. The evil of having slaves was experienced during the late war. Had slaves been treated as they might have been by the enemy, they would have proved dangerous instruments in their hands. But their folly dealt by the slaves, as it did by the Tories. He mentioned the dangerous insurrections of the slaves in Greece and Sicily and the instructions given . . . to the commissioners sent to Virginia, to arm the servants and slaves, in case other means of obtaining its submission should fail. Maryland and Virginia, he said, had already prohibited the importation of slaves expressly. North Carolina had done the same in substance. All this would be in vain if South Carolina and Georgia be at liberty to import. The Western people are already calling out for slaves for their new lands and will fill the country with slaves if they can be got through South Carolina and Georgia. Slavery discourages arts and manufactures. The poor despise labor when performed by slaves. They prevent the immigration of whites, who really enrich and strengthen a country. They produce the most pernicious effect on manners. Every master of slaves is born a petty tyrant. They bring the judgment of heaven on a country. As nations can not be rewarded or punished in the next world, they must be in this. By an inevitable chain of causes and effects providence punishes national sins by national calamities. He lamented that some of our eastern brethren had, from a lust of gain, embarked in this nefarious traffic. As to the states being in possession of the right to import, this was the case with many other rights, now to be properly given up. He held it essential in every point of view that the general government should have power to prevent the increase of slavery.

MR. ELSWORTH. As he had never owned a slave could not judge of the effects of slavery on character. He said, however, that if it was to be considered in a moral light, we ought to go farther and free those already in the country. As slaves also multiply so fast in Virginia and Maryland that it is cheaper to raise than import them whilst in the sickly rice swamps foreign supplies are necessary, if we go no farther than is urged, we shall be unjust towards South Carolina and Georgia. Let us not intermeddle. As population increases, poor laborers will be so plenty as to render slaves useless. Slavery in time will not be a speck in our country. Provision is already made in Connecticut for abolishing it. And the abolition has already taken place in Massachusetts. As to the danger of insurrections from foreign influence, that will become a motive to kind treatment of the slaves.

Potential Consequences of Barring Slavery

MR. PINKNEY. If slavery be wrong, it is justified by the example of all the world. He cited the case of Greece, Rome and other ancient states and the sanction given by France, England, Holland and other modern states. In all ages one half of mankind have been slaves. If the southern states were let alone they will probably of themselves stop importations. He would himself, as a citizen of South Carolina, vote for it. An attempt to take away the right as proposed will produce serious objections to the Constitution which he wished to see adopted.

GEN. [CHARLES] PINKNEY declared it to be his firm opinion that if himself and all his colleagues were to sign the Constitution & use their personal influence, it would be of no avail towards obtaining the assent of their constituents. South Carolina and Georgia cannot do without slaves. As to Virginia she will gain by stopping the importations. Her slaves will rise in value, and she has more than she wants.

It would be unequal to require South Carolina and Georgia to confederate on such unequal terms. He said the royal assent before the Revolution had never been refused to South Carolina as to Virginia. He contended that the importation of slaves would be for the interest of the whole Union. The more slaves, the more produce to employ the carrying trade. The more consumption also, and the more of his, the more of revenue for the common treasury. He admitted it to be reasonable that slaves should be dutied like other imports, but should consider a rejection of the clause as an exclusion of South Carolina from the Union.

MR. [ABRAHAM] BALDWIN had conceived national objects alone to be before the Convention, not . . . like the present [which] were of a local nature. Georgia was decided on this point. That state has always hitherto supposed a general government to be the pursuit of the central states who wished to have a vortex for every thing—that her distance would preclude her from equal advantage—and that she could not prudently purchase it by yielding national powers. From this it might be understood in what light she would view an attempt to abridge one of her favorite prerogatives. If left to herself, she may probably put a stop to the evil. . . .

MR. [JAMES] WILSON observed that if South Carolina and Georgia were themselves disposed to get rid of the importation of slaves in a short time as had been suggested, they would never refuse to unite because the importation might be prohibited. As the section now stands, all articles imported are to be taxed. Slaves alone are exempt. This is in fact a bounty on that article.

MR. GERRY thought we had nothing to do with the conduct of the states as to slaves, but ought to be careful not to give any sanction to it.

MR. [JOHN] DICKINSON considered it as inadmissible on every principle of honor & safety that the importation of slaves should be authorised to the states by the Constitution. The true question was whether the national happiness would be promoted or impeded by the importation, and this question ought to be left to the national government not to the states particularly interested. If England and France permit slavery, slaves are at the same time excluded from both those kingdoms. Greece and Rome were made unhappy by their slaves. He could not believe that the southern states would refuse to confederate on the account apprehended, especially as the power was not likely to be immediately exercised by the general government.

MR. WILLIAMSON stated the law of North Carolina on the subject . . . did not directly prohibit the importation of slaves. It imposed a duty of £5 on each slave imported from Africa, £10 on each from elsewhere and £50 on each from a state licensing manumission. He thought the southern states could not be members of the Union if the clause should be rejected, and that it was wrong to force any thing down, not absolutely necessary, and which any state must disagree to.

The Hope for Middle Ground

MR. KING thought the subject should be considered in a political light only. If two states will not agree to the Constitution as stated on one side, he could affirm with equal belief on the other that great and equal opposition would be experienced from the other states. He remarked on the exemption of slaves from duty whilst every other import was subjected to it as an inequality that could not fail to strike the commercial sagacity of the north and Middle states.

MR. [JOHN] LANGDON was strenuous for giving the power to the general government. He could not with a good conscience leave it with the states who could then go on with the traffic, without being restrained by the opinions here given that they will themselves cease to import slaves.

GEN. PINKNEY thought himself bound to declare candidly that he did not think South Carolina would stop her importations of slaves in any short time, but only stop them occasionally as she now does. He moved to commit the clause that slaves might be made liable to an equal tax with other imports, which he thought right & which would remove one difficulty that had been started.

MR. RUTLEDGE: If the Convention thinks that North Carolina, South Carolina and Georgia will ever agree to the plan, unless their right to import slaves be untouched, the expectation is vain. The people of those states will never be such fools as to give up so important an interest. He was strenuous against striking out the section and seconded the motion of General Pinkney for a commitment.

MR. MORRIS wished the whole subject to be committed including the clauses relating to taxes on exports and to a navigation–act. These things may form a bargain between the northern and southern states.

MR. BUTLER declared that he never would agree to the power of taxing exports.

MR. SHERMAN said it was better to let the southern states import slaves than to part with them if they made that a sine qua non. He was opposed to a tax on slaves imported as making the matter worse because it implied they were *property*. He acknowledged that if the power of prohibiting the importation should be given to the general government that it would be exercised. He thought it would be its duty to exercise the power.

MR. [GEORGE] READ was for the commitment provided the clause concerning taxes on exports should also be committed. . . .

MR. [EDMUND] RANDOLPH was for committing in order that some middle ground might, if possible, be found. He could never agree to the clause as it stands. He would sooner risk the constitution. He dwelt on the dilemma to which the Convention was exposed. By agreeing to the clause, it would revolt the Quakers, the Methodists and many others in the States having no slaves. On the other hand, two States might be lost to the Union. Let us then, he said, try the chance of a commitment.

Chapter 4

Reactions to the Finished Product

Chapter Preface

There were many reasons why someone might have liked or disliked the system of government proposed in the U.S. Constitution. However, because the immediate decision was only whether to ratify the document, the debate essentially boiled down to two broad camps. On one side were the Federalists, who argued in favor of ratification of the Constitution. On the other side of the debate were the Anti-Federalists, who opposed ratification. The Federalists had an immediate advantage in the debate simply by being able to claim the name *Federalists*. They could argue that they were attempting to solve the problems of the Articles of Confederation. The Federalists were also helped in their campaign for public acceptance of the Constitution because they were led by the delegates who attended the Constitutional Convention. Being led by the political elite could also be a liability for the Federalists, however. First, Anti-Federalists could whip up antagonism toward the Constitution by arguing that the political elite were not taking into account the needs and desires of the "common folk." Further, the delegates to the Constitutional Convention were used to the high politics that often (but not always) marked debate in the convention rather than the low politics that typically dominated debate in the state conventions or in the war of words that raged in the newspapers across the country.

The Federalists encouraged people to believe that the Anti-Federalists had no other solutions beyond rejecting the Constitution. However, in many ways the Anti-Federalists suffered from having too many solutions. The Anti-Federalists could never agree among themselves what they wanted to do if the Constitution were rejected. Some suggested that the United States should break up into three or four smaller countries. Others felt that the country should continue to use the Articles of Confederation. Still others believed that changes should be made to strengthen the Articles of Confederation but the Constitution went too far in granting undue authority to the national government.

In the end, the Federalists won the ratification debate. However, the vigorous attacks made by the Anti-Federalists strengthened the Constitution and the nation at such a critical juncture in history. By forcing the supporters of the Constitution to debate publicly about the reasons why they supported the Constitution, the debate dispelled misgivings that people had about the secrecy that surrounded the convention.

Current generations are thankful for these debates, which were carried out in newspapers, pamphlets, and state conventions in all thirteen states, because they provide a better understanding of what the framers of the U.S. Constitution intended to do when they wrote the document in a particular way. Perhaps the most important of these are the eighty-five articles collectively called *The Federalist Papers,* by Alexander Hamilton, James Madison, and John Jay, written primarily to persuade a skeptical New York State to ratify the Constitution. These articles are certainly political propaganda. However, as two of the authors (Hamilton and Madison) were active delegates in the convention, these writings also represent some of the best examples of early American political philosophy.

The Father of the Constitution Takes Stock

James Madison

> James Madison is often called the "Father of the U.S. Constitution." He certainly played an active role throughout the Convention and many of his ideas were instituted as part of the final document. An equally important historical contribution has been the copious notes that James Madison took of the debates during the Constitutional Convention. These notes certainly helped him in writing this letter of October 24, 1787, to Thomas Jefferson, who was in France as the American ambassador. Madison is able to describe concisely the fundamental debates that transpired during the Convention. He ends his letter with his assessment of the chances of ratification of the Constitution in the various states, with particular emphasis on the politics of ratification in his (and Jefferson's) home state of Virginia.

You will herewith receive the result of the Convention, which continued its session till the 17th of September. I take the liberty of making some observations on the subject which will help to make up a letter, if they should answer no other purpose.

It appeared to be the sincere and unanimous wish of the Convention to cherish and preserve the Union of the States. No proposition was made, no suggestion was thrown

From James Madison's October 24, 1787, letter to Thomas Jefferson, as reprinted in *The Papers of James Madison,* vol. 10, *27 May 1787–3 March 1788,* edited by Robert Rutland et al. (Chicago: University of Chicago Press, 1977).

out, in favor of a partition of the Empire into two or more confederacies.

It was generally agreed that the objects of the Union could not be secured by any system founded on the principle of a confederation of sovereign states. A *voluntary* observance of the federal law by all the members, could never be hoped for. A *compulsive* one could evidently never be reduced to practice, and if it could, involved equal calamities to the innocent & the guilty, the necessity of a military force both obnoxious and dangerous, and in general, a scene resembling much more a civil war, than the administration of a regular government.

Hence was embraced the alternative of a government which, instead of operating on the states, should operate without their intervention on the individuals composing them: and hence the change in the principle and proportion of representation.

This ground-work being laid, the great objects which presented themselves were 1. to unite a proper energy in the Executive and a proper stability in the legislative departments, with the essential characters of republican government. 2. To draw a line of demarcation which would give to the general government every power requisite for general purposes and leave to the States every power which might be most beneficially administered by them. 3. To provide for the different interests of different parts of the Union. 4. To adjust the clashing pretensions of the large and small states. Each of these objects was pregnant with difficulties. The whole of them together formed a task more difficult than can be well conceived by those who were not concerned in the execution of it. Adding to these considerations the natural diversity of human opinions on all new and complicated subjects, it is impossible to consider the degree of concord which ultimately prevailed as less than a miracle.

Settling the Executive Debate

The first of these objects as it respects the Executive, was peculiarly embarrassing. On the question whether it should consist of a single person or a plurality of co-ordinate members: on the mode of appointment; on the duration in office; on the degree of power and on the re-eligibility, tedious and reiterated discussions took place. The plurality of co-ordinate members had finally but few advocates. Governor [Edmund] Randolph was at the head of them. The modes of appointment proposed were various, as by the people at large—by electors chosen by the people—by the Executives of the States—by the Congress, some preferring a joint ballot of the two Houses—some a separate concurrent ballot allowing to each a negative on the other house—some a nomination of several candidates by one House, out of whom a choice should be made by the other. Several other modifications were started. The expedient at length adopted seemed to give pretty general satisfaction to the members. As to the duration in office, a few would have preferred a tenure during good behavior—a considerable number would have done so, in case an easy and effectual removal by impeachment could be settled. It was much agitated whether a long term, seven years for example, with a subsequent and perpetual ineligibility, or a short term with a capacity to be re-elected, should be fixed. In favor of the first opinion were urged the danger of a gradual degeneracy of re-elections from time to time, into first life and then a heriditary tenure, and the favorable effect of an incapacity to be reappointed, on the independent exercise of the executive authority. On the other side it was contended that the prospect of necessary degradation would discourage the most dignified characters from aspiring to the office, would take away the principal motive to the faithful discharge of its duties—the hope of being rewarded with a reappointment, would stimulate ambition to violent efforts for holding over the constitutional term—and instead of producing an independent administration, and a firmer defence of the constitutional rights of the department, would render the officer more indifferent to the importance of a place which he would soon be obliged to quit forever, and more ready to yield to the encroachments of the legislature of which he might again be a member. The questions concerning the degree of power turned chiefly on the appointment to offices and the control on the legislature. An *absolute* appointment to all offices—to some offices—to no offices, formed the scale of opinions on the first point. On the second, some contended for an absolute negative as the only possible mean of reducing to practice the theory of a free government which forbids a mixture of the legislative and executive powers. Others would be content with a revisionary power to be overruled by three-fourths of both Houses. It was warmly urged that the judiciary department should be associated in the revision. The idea of some was that a separate revision should be given to the two departments—that if either objected two-thirds; if both three-fourths, should be necessary to overrule.

Congress and Its Powers

In forming the Senate, the great anchor of the government, the questions as they came within the first object turned mostly on the mode of appointment, and the duration of it. The different modes proposed were, 1. by the House of Representatives 2. by the Executive, 3. by electors chosen by the people for the purpose. 4. by the state legislatures. On the point of duration, the propositions descended from good-behavior to four years, through the intermediate terms of nine, seven, six, & five years. The election of the other branch was first determined to be triennial, and afterwards reduced to biennial.

The second object, the due partition of power, between the general & local governments, was perhaps of all, the most nice and difficult. A few contended for an entire abolition of the states; some for indefinite power of legislation in the Congress, with a negative on the laws of the states: some for such a power without a negative; some for a limited power of legislation, with such a negative. The majority [was] finally for a limited power without the negative. The question with regard to the negative underwent repeated discussions and was finally rejected by a bare majority. As I formerly intimated to you my opinion in favor of this ingredient, I will take this occasion of explaining myself on the subject. Such a check on the states appears to me necessary 1. to prevent encroachments on the general authority. 2. to prevent instability and injustice in the legislation of the states.

James Madison

1. Without such a check in the whole over the parts, our system involves the evil of imperia in imperio. If a complete supremacy some where is not necessary in every society, a controling power at least is so, by which the general authority may be defended against encroachments of the subordinate authorities, and by which the latter may be restrained from encroachments on each other. . . .

Still more to the purpose is our own experience both during the war and since the peace. Encroachments of the states on the general authority, sacrifices of national to local interests, interferences of the measures of different States, form a great part of the history of our political system. It may be said that the new Constitution is founded on different principles and will have a different operation. I admit the difference to the material. It presents the aspect rather of a feudal system of republics, if such a phrase may be used, than of a Confederacy of independent States. And what has been the progress and event of the feudal constitutions? In all of them a continual struggle between the head and the inferior members, until a final victory has been gained in some instances by one, in others, by the other of them. In one respect indeed there is remarkable variance between the two cases. In the feudal system the sovereign, though limited, was independent, and having no particular sympathy of interests with the great Barons, his ambition had as full play as theirs in the mutual projects of usurpation. In the American Constitution, the general authority will be derived entirely from the subordinate authorities. The Senate will represent the states in their political capacity; the other House will represent the people of the states in their individual capac[it]y. The former will be accountable to their constituents at moderate, the latter at short periods. The President also derives his appointment from the States, and is periodically accountable to them. This dependence of the general on the local authorities seems effectually to guard the latter against any dangerous encroachments of the former. The latter, within their respective limits, will be continually sensible of the abridgment of their power and be stimulated by ambition to resume the surrendered portion of it.

Some contended for an unlimited power over trade including exports as well as imports, and over slaves as well as other imports; some for such a power, provided the concurrence of two-thirds of both House were required; some for such a qualification of the power, with an exemption of exports and slaves; others for an exemption of exports only. The result is seen in the Constitution. South Carolina and Georgia were inflexible on the point of the slaves.

State Representation in Congress

The remaining object created more embarrassment and a greater alarm for the issue of the Convention than all the rest put together. The little states insisted on retaining their equality in both branches, unless a compleat abolition of the state governments should take place, and made an equality in the Senate a sine qua non. The large states on the other hand urged that, as the new government was to be drawn principally from the people immediately and was to operate directly on them, not on the States, and, consequently, as the States would lose that importance which is now proportioned to the importance of their voluntary compliances with the requisitions of Congress, it was necessary that the representation in both Houses should be in proportion to their size. It ended in the compromise which you will see, but very much to the dissatisfaction of several members from the large states.

Some Virginia Dissenters

It will not escape you that three names only from Virginia are subscribed to the Act. Mr. [George] Wythe did not return after the death of his lady. Dr. [James] McClurg left the Convention some time before the adjournment. The Governor [Edmund Randolph] and Col. [George] Mason refused to be parties to it. Mr. [Elbridge] Gerry was the only other member who refused. The objections of the Governor turn principally on the latitude of the general powers and on the connection established between the President and the Senate. He wished that the plan should be proposed to the states with liberty to them to suggest alterations which should all be referred to another general Convention, to be incorporated into the plan as far as might be judged expedient. He was not inveterate in his opposition and grounded his refusal to subscribe pretty much on his unwillingness to commit himself, so as not to be at liberty to be governed by further lights on the subject. Col. Mason left Philadelphia in an exceeding ill-humor indeed. A number of little circumstances arising in part from the impatience which prevailed towards the close of the business conspired to whet his acrimony. He returned to Virginia with a fixed disposition to prevent the adoption of the plan if possible. He considers the want of a Bill of Rights as a fatal objection. His other objections are to the substitution of the Senate in place of an Executive Council and to the powers vested in that body—to the powers of the Judiciary—to the Vice President being made President of the Senate—to the smallness of the number of Representatives—to the restriction on the states with regard to ex post facto laws—and most of all probably to the power of regulating trade by a majority only of each House. He has some other lesser objections. Being now under the necessity of justifying his refusal to sign, he will, of course, muster every possible one. His conduct has given great umbrage to the County of Fairfax, and particularly to the town of Alexandria. He is already instructed to promote in the Assembly the calling a Convention and will probably be either not deputed to the Convention or be tied up by express instructions. He did not object in general to the powers vested in the national government so much as to the modification. In some respects he admitted that some further powers would have improved the system. He acknowledged, in particular, that a negative on the state laws and the appointment of the state executives ought to be ingredients, but supposed that the public mind would not now bear them, and that experience would hereafter produce these amendments.

Adoption of the Plan Is Expected

The final reception which will be given by the people at large to the proposed System can not yet be decided. The legislature of New Hampshire was sitting when it reached that state and was well pleased with it. As far as the sense of the people there has been expressed, it is equally favorable. Boston is warm and almost unanimous in embracing it. The impression [in] the country is not yet known. No symptoms of disapprobation have appeared. The legislature of that state is now sitting, through which the sense of the people at large will soon be promulged with tolerable certainty. The paper money faction in Rhode Island is hostile. The other party zealously attached to it. Its passage through Connecticut is likely to be very smooth and easy. There seems to be less agitation in this state than any where. The discussion of the subject seems confined to the newspapers. The principal characters are known to be friendly. The Governor's party, which has hitherto been the popular and most numerous one, is supposed to be on the opposite side, but considerable reserve is practised, of which he sets the example. New Jersey takes the affirmative side, of course. Meetings of the people are declaring their approbation and instructing their representatives. Pennsylvania will be divided. The City of Philadelphia, the Republican Party, the Quakers and most of the Germans espouse the Constitution. Some of the Constitutional leaders, backed by the western country will oppose.

An unlucky ferment on the subject in their Assembly just before its late adjournment has irritated both sides, particularly the opposition and, by redoubling the exertions of that party, may render the event doubtful. The voice of Maryland, I understand from pretty good authority, is, as far as it has been declared, strongly in favor of the Constitution. . . . My information from Virginia is, as yet, extremely imperfect. I have a letter from General Washington, which speaks favorably of the impression within a circle of some extent and another from Chancellor [Edmund] Pendleton, which expresses his full acceptance of the plan and the popularity of it in his district. I am told also that [Harry] Innis and [John] Marshall are patrons of it. In the opposite scale are Mr. James Mercer, Mr. Richard Henry Lee . . . and most of the judges and bar of the General Court. The part which Mr. [Patrick] Henry will take is unknown here. Much will depend on it. I had taken it for granted from a variety of circumstances that he would be in the opposition and still think that will be the case. There are reports however which favor a contrary supposition. From the States South of Virginia nothing has been heard. As the deputation from South Carolina consisted of some of its weightiest characters, who have returned unanimously zealous in favor to the Constitution, it is probable that state will readily embrace it. It is not less probable, that North Carolina will follow the example, unless that of Virginia should counterbalance it. Upon the whole, although, the public mind will not be fully known, nor finally settled for a considerable time, appearances at present augur a more prompt, and general adoption of the plan than could have been well expected.

An American in Paris Reacts

Thomas Jefferson

Thomas Jefferson, the author of the Declaration of Independence, did not attend the Constitutional Convention because he was in Paris, serving as the American ambassador to France. However, his absence does not imply that he was disinterested in the struggle to write the Constitution or in the final product. On December 20, 1787, Thomas Jefferson wrote this letter to James Madison, the often-described Father of the U.S. Constitution. In the letter, he describes what he likes (e.g., separation of powers, taxation powers to Congress, veto power to the president) and what he dislikes (e.g., omission of a Bill of Rights, the direct election of the president, and, most importantly, the impression that the Constitution creates, in his words, "a very energetic government"). By the end, it is clear that Thomas Jefferson is not a fan of the U.S. Constitution.

The season admitting only of operations in the Cabinet, and these being in a great measure secret, I have little to fill a letter. I will therefore make up the deficiency by adding a few words on the Constitution proposed by our convention. I like much the general idea of framing a government which should go on of itself peaceably, without needing continual recurrence to the state legislatures. I like the organization of the government into legislative, judiciary and executive. I like the power given the legislature to levy

From Thomas Jefferson's December 20, 1787, letter to James Madison, as reprinted in *The Papers of Thomas Jefferson,* vol. 12, *7 August 1787 to 31 March 1788,* edited by Julian Boyd (Princeton, NJ: Princeton University Press, 1955).

taxes and for that reason solely approve of the greater house being chosen by the people directly. For though I think a house chosen by them will be very ill-qualified to legislate for the Union, for foreign nations etc., yet this evil does not weigh against the good of preserving inviolate the fundamental principle that the people are not to be taxed but by representatives chosen immediately by themselves. I am captivated by the compromise of the opposite claims of the great and little states, of the latter to equal and the former to proportional influence. I am much pleased too with the substitution of the method of voting by persons, instead of voting by states. And I like the negative given to the Executive with a third of either house, though I should have liked it better had the judiciary been associated for that purpose, or invested with a similar and separate power. There are other good things of less moment. I will now add what I do not like. First the omission of a bill of rights providing clearly and without the aid of sophisms for freedom of religion, freedom of the press, protection against standing armies, restriction against monopolies, the eternal and unremitting force of the habeas corpus laws, and trials by jury in all matters of fact triable by the laws of the land and not by the law of nations.

The Need for a Bill of Rights

To say, as Mr. [James] Wilson does that a bill of rights was not necessary because all is reserved in the case of the general government which is not given, while in the particular ones all is given which is not reserved might do for the audience to whom it was addressed, but [it] is surely gratis dictum, opposed by strong inferences from the body of the instrument, as well as from the omission of the clause of our present confederation which had declared that in express terms. It was a hard conclusion to say [that] because there has been no uniformity among the states as to the cases triable by jury [and] because some have been so incautious as to abandon this mode of trial, therefore, the more prudent states shall be reduced to the same level of calamity. It

would have been much more just and wise to have conclud-
ed the other way that as most of the states had judiciously
preserved this palladium, those who had wandered should
be brought back to it, and to have established general right
instead of general wrong. Let me add that a bill of rights is
what the people are entitled to against every government on
earth, general or particular, and what no just government
should refuse, or rest on inference.

American Monarchy

The second feature I dislike, and greatly dislike, is the abandonment in every instance of the necessity of rotation in office, and most particularly in the case of the President. Experience concurs with reason in concluding that the first
magistrate will always be re-elected if the constitution per-
mits it. He is then an officer for life. This once observed it
becomes of so much consequence to certain nations to have
a friend or a foe at the head of our affairs that they will interfere with money and with arms. A Galloman [French-
man] or an Angloman [Englishman] will be supported by
the nation he befriends. If once elected, and at a second or
third election outvoted by one or two votes, he will pretend
false votes, foul play, hold possession of the reins of government, be supported by the states voting for him, especially if they are the central ones lying in a compact body
themselves and separating their opponents; and they will be
aided by one nation of Europe, while the majority are aided by another. The election of a President of America some
years hence will be much more interesting to certain nations
of Europe than ever the election of a king of Poland was.
Reflect on all the instances in history ancient and modern,
of elective monarchies, and say if they do not give foundation for my fears, the Roman emperors, the popes, while
they were of any importance, the German emperors till they
became hereditary in practice, the kings of Poland, the Deys
of the Ottoman dependancies. It may be said that if elections
are to be attended with these disorders, the less seldom they
are renewed the better. But experience shows that the only

way to prevent disorder is to render them uninteresting by frequent changes. An incapacity to be elected a second time would have been the only effectual preventative. The power of removing him every fourth year by the vote of the people is a power which will not be exercised. The king of Poland is removeable every day by the Diet [their legislature], yet he is never removed. Smaller objections are the appeal in fact as well as law and the binding [of] all persons legislative, executive and judiciary by oath to maintain that constitution.

No Friend to an Energetic Government

I do not pretend to decide what would be the best method of procuring the establishment of the manifold good things in this constitution, and of getting rid of the bad. Whether by adopting it in hopes of future amendment, or, after it has been duly weighed and canvassed by the people, after seeing the parts they generally dislike, and those they generally approve, to say to them 'We see now what you wish. Send together your deputies again, let them frame a constitution for you omitting what you have condemned, and establishing the powers you approve. Even these will be a great addition to the energy of your government.' At all events I hope you will not be discouraged from other trials, if the present one should fail of its full effect. I have thus told you freely what I like and dislike—merely as a matter of curiosity for I know your own judgment has been formed on all these points after having heard every thing which could be urged on them. I won I am not a friend to a very energetic government. It is always oppressive. The late rebellion in Massachusetts [Shays' Rebellion] has given more alarm than I think it should have done. Calculate that one rebellion in 13 states in the course of 11 years is but one for each state in a century and a half. No country should be so long without one. Nor will any degree of power in the hands of government prevent insurrections. France with all its despotism, and two or three hundred thousand men always in arms has had three insurrections in the three years I have

been here—in every one of which greater numbers were engaged than in Massachusetts and a great deal more blood
was spilt. In Turkey, which Montesquieu supposes more
despotic, insurrections are the events of every day. In England, where the hand of power is lighter than here, but
heavier than with us, they happen every half dozen years.
Compare again the ferocious depredations of their insurgents with the order, the moderation and the almost self ex-
tinguishment of ours. After all, it is my principle that the
will of the majority should always prevail. If they approve
the proposed Convention in all its parts, I shall concur in it
cheerfully, in hopes that they will amend it whenever they
shall find it work wrong. I think our governments will remain virtuous for many centuries (as long as they are chiefly
agricultural), and this will be as long as there shall be va-
cant lands in any part of America. When they get piled upon
one another in large cities, as in Europe, they will become
corrupt as in Europe. Above all things I hope the education
of the common people will be attended to; [I am] convinced
that on their good sense we may rely with the most security for the preservation of a due degree of liberty. I have tired
you by this time with my disquisitions and will therefore
only add assurances of the sincerity of those sentiments of
esteem and attachment with which I am, Dear Sir, your affectionate friend and servant.

A List of Faults of the Constitution

Anonymous

After the Constitution was made public, newspapers began running letters to the editor and op-ed pieces in which they described their support for or opposition to the proposed plan of government. This anonymous article appeared in the *Massachusetts Centinel* on November 21, 1787 (about a month after the Constitutional Convention finished its work). The author, who remains anonymous, provides the reader with a list of problems—both great and small—with the U.S. Constitution. Many of this author's complaints seem to stem from the fact that the Constitution did not include a Bill of Rights, which would have protected trial by jury, freedom of the press, and other liberties.

The following objections made to the new Constitution you are requested to publish for the consideration of the public at this all-important crisis. Yours, Anonymous.

The objections that have been made to the new Constitution are these:

1. It is not merely (as it ought to be) a confederation of states, but a government of individuals.

2. The powers of Congress extend to the lives, the liberties and the property of every citizen.

3. The sovereignty of the different states is *ipso facto* destroyed in its most essential parts.

From Anonymous, "A List of Faults of the United States Constitution," *Massachusetts Centinel*, November 21, 1787.

4. What remains of it will only tend to create violent dissensions between the state governments and the Congress and terminate in the ruin of the one or the other.

5. The consequence must therefore be, either that the union of the states will be destroyed by a violent struggle or that their sovereignty will be swallowed up by silent encroachments into a universal aristocracy because it is clear that if two different sovereign powers have a co-equal command over the purses of the citizens, they will struggle for the spoils, and the weakest will be in the end obliged to yield to the efforts of the strongest.

6. Congress being possessed of these immense powers, the liberties of the states and of the people are not secured by a bill or Declaration of Rights.

7. The sovereignty of the states is not expressly reserved; the form only, and not the substance of their government, is guaranteed to them by express words.

8. Trial by jury, that sacred bulwark of liberty, is abolished in civil cases, and Mr. [James] Wilson, one of the convention, has told you that not being able to agree as to the form of establishing this point, they have left you deprived of the substance. . . . The convention found the task too difficult for them and left the business as it stands.

9. The liberty of the press is not secured and the powers of Congress are fully adequate to its destruction as they are to have the trial of libels, or pretended libels, against the United States, and [there] may be a cursed abominable stamp act (as the Bowdoin administration has done in Massachusetts) [to] preclude you effectually from all means of information. Mr. Wilson has given you no answer to these arguments.

10. Congress have the power of keeping up a standing army in the time of peace, and Mr. Wilson has told you that it was necessary.

11. The legislative and executive powers are not kept separate as every one of the American constitutions declares they ought to be, but they are mixed in a manner entirely novel and unknown, even to the constitution of Great Britain; because,

12. In England the king only has a nominal negative over the proceedings of the legislature, which he has never dared to exer-

cise since the days of King William, whereas by the new Constitution, both the President and the Senate, two executive branches of government, have that negative and are intended to support each other in the exercise of it.

13. The representation of the lower house is too small, consisting only of sixty-five members.

14. That the Senate is so small that it renders its extensive powers extremely dangerous. It is to consist only of twenty-six members, two-thirds of whom must concur to conclude any treaty or alliance with foreign powers. Now we will suppose that five of them absent, sick, dead or unable to attend, twenty-one will remain, and eight of these (one-third and one over) may prevent the conclusion of any treaty, even the most favorable to America. Here will be a fine field for the intrigues and even the bribery and corruption of European powers.

15. The most important branches of the executive department are to be put into the hands of a single magistrate who will be in fact an elective king. The military, the land and naval forces are to be entirely at his disposal, and therefore:

16. Should the Senate, by the intrigues of foreign powers, become devoted to foreign influence, as was the case of late in Sweden, the people will be obliged, as the Swedes have been, to seek their refuge in the arms of the monarch or President.

17. Rotation, that noble prerogative of liberty, is entirely excluded from the new system of government, and great men may and probably will be continued in office during their lives.

18. Annual elections are abolished, and the people are not to reassume their rights until the expiration of two, four, and six years.

19. Congress are to have the power of fixing the time, place, and manner of holding elections, so as to keep them forever subjected to their influence.

20. The importation of slaves is not to be prohibited until the year 1808, and slavery will probably resume its empire in all the states.

21. The militia is to be under the immediate command of Congress, and men conscientiously scrupulous of bearing arms, may be compelled to perform military duty.

22. The new government will be expensive beyond any we have ever experienced. The judicial department alone, with its concomitant train of judges, justices, chancellors, clerks, sheriffs, coroners, state attorneys and solicitors, constables, etc., in every state and in every county in each state, will be a burden beyond the utmost abilities of the people to bear, and upon the whole.

23. A government partaking of monarchy and aristocracy will be fully and firmly established, and liberty will be but a name to adorn the short historic page of the halcyon days of America.

These, my countrymen, are the objections that have been made to the new proposed system of government, and if you read the system itself with attention, you will find them all to be founded in truth.

An Antifederalist Attack on the Constitution

The Federal Farmer

Signed with the anonymous title "The Federal Farmer," a series of eighteen letters critical of the Constitution are often attributed to Richard Henry Lee. Richard Henry Lee was a prominent Virginia critic of the Constitution. As a delegate to the Continental Congress from Virginia, he felt it was improper for himself to accept a position on the Virginia delegation to the Constitutional Convention. Attributing these eighteen letters, which were written from October 8, 1787, until January 25, 1788, and then collected in two widely read pamphlets, to Lee is primarily supported by two arguments. First, a letter hostile to the Federal Farmer's first letter was published in the *Connecticut Courant,* which identified Lee as the Federal Farmer. Second, many of the ideas in these letters reflect Lee's primary criticisms of the Constitution, which he made public in the Continental Congress debates of the Constitution on September 26–28, 1787. Despite this solid evidence, Richard Henry Lee's authorship is not definitive because Lee never acknowledged, either in public or in private letters to friends, that he had written the letters.

The bulk of the letters were written in anticipation of the states meeting to debate possible ratification of the Constitution. They are addressed to "The Republican"—any citizen

From Anonymous (Richard H. Lee), *Observations Leading to a Fair Examination of the System of Government Proposed by the Late Convention* (New York: T. Greenleaf, 1787).

concerned with the creation of a new government. The letter presented here is the Federal Farmer's fifth, written on October 13. In it, the Federal Farmer critically analyzes the proposed system of government under the Constitution. While not rejecting the Constitution entirely, the Federal Farmer finds enough fault with it that he recommends that it be amended.

One particular concern is that the Constitution creates a government that privileges wealthy aristocrats. He believes that wealthy politicians dominated the Constitutional Convention and created a system of government suited to protect their interests rather than a system of government that properly balances power between the national government and state governments and protects individual rights. At the very least, he recommends that the states take a long, hard look at the document and propose changes to those parts of the Constitution that they do not like before agreeing to it.

D ear Sir, Thus I have examined the federal constitution as far as a few days leisure would permit. It opens to my mind a new scene; instead of seeing powers cautiously lodged in the hands of numerous legislators and many magistrates, we see all important powers collecting in one center, where a few men will possess them almost at discretion. And instead of checks in the formation of the government, to secure the rights of the people against the usurpations of those they appoint to govern, we are to understand the equal division of lands among our people and the strong arm furnished them by nature and situation are to secure them against those usurpations. If there are advantages in the equal division of our lands and the strong and manly habits of our people, we ought to establish governments calculated to give duration to them and not governments which never can work naturally till that equality of property and those free and manly habits shall be destroyed; these evidently are not the natural basis of the proposed constitution. No man of reflection and skilled in the science of government can suppose these will move on harmoniously together for ages or even for fifty years. As to the little circumstances commented upon, by some writers, with applause—as the age of a representative, of the president, &c.—they have, in my mind, no weight in the general tendency of the system.

There are, however, in my opinion, many good things in the proposed system. It is founded on elective principles, and the deposits of powers in different hands is essentially right. The guards against those evils we have experienced in some states in legislation are valuable indeed, but the value of every feature in this system is vastly lessened for the want of that one important feature in a free government, a representation of the people. Because we have sometimes abused democracy, I am not among those men who think a democratic branch a nuisance; which branch shall be sufficiently numerous, to admit some of the best informed men of each order in the community into the administration of government.

While the radical defects in the proposed system are not so soon discovered, some temptations to each state and to many classes of men to adopt it are very visible. It uses the democratic language of several of the state constitutions, particularly that of Massachusetts; the eastern states will receive advantages so far as the regulation of trade, by a bare majority, is committed to it. Connecticut and New Jersey will receive their share of a general impost. The middle states will receive the advantages surrounding the seat of government. The southern states will receive protection and have their negroes represented in the legislature and large back countries will soon have a majority in it. This system promises a large field of employment to military gentlemen and gentlemen of the law; and in case the government shall be executed without convulsions, it will afford security to creditors, to the clergy, salaried men and others depending on money payments. So far as the system promises justice and reasonable advantages, in these respects, it ought to be supported by all honest men; but whenever it promises unequal and improper advantages to any particular states, or orders of men, it ought to be opposed.

A Warning Against Haste

I have in the course of these letters observed that there are many good things in the proposed constitution, and I have endeavored to point out many important defects in it. I have admitted that we want a federal system—that we have a system presented, which, with several alterations may be made a tolerable good one—I have admitted there is a well founded uneasiness among creditors and mercantile men. In this situation of things, you ask me what I think ought to be done? My opinion in this case is only the opinion of an individual, and so far only as it corresponds with the opinions of the honest and substantial part of the community is it entitled to consideration. Though I am fully satisfied that the state conventions ought most seriously to direct their exertions to altering and amending the system proposed before they shall adopt it—yet I have not sufficiently examined the subject, or formed an opinion, how far it will be practicable for those conventions to carry their amendments. As to the idea that it will be in vain for those conventions to attempt amendments, it cannot be admitted; it is impossible to say whether they can or not until the attempt shall be made. When it shall be determined by experience that the conventions cannot agree in amendments, it will then be an important question before the people of the United States, whether they will adopt or not the system proposed in its present form. This subject of consolidating the states is new; and because forty or fifty men have agreed in a system, to suppose the good sense of this country, an enlightened nation, must adopt it without examination and though in a state of profound peace, without endeavouring to amend those parts they perceive are defective, dangerous to freedom and destructive of the valuable principles of republican government—is truly humiliating. It is true there may be danger in delay, but there is danger in adopting the system in its present form, and I see the danger in either case will arise principally from the conduct and views of two very unprincipled parties in the United States—two fires, between which the honest and substantial people have long found themselves situated.

Class Politics

One party is composed of little insurgents, men in debt, who want no law, and who want a share of the property of others; these are called levellers, Shayites [supporters of Shays' Rebellion], &c. The other party is composed of a few, but more dangerous men, with their servile dependents; these avariciously grasp at all power and property. You may discover in all the actions of these men, an evident dislike to free and equal government, and they will go systematically to work to change, essentially, the forms of government in this country. These are called aristocrats. . . . Between these two parties is the weight of the community, the men of middling property, men not in debt on the one hand, and men, on the other, content with republican governments, and not aiming at immense fortunes, offices and power. In 1786, the little insurgents, the levellers, came forth, invaded the rights of others and attempted to establish governments according to their wills. Their movements evidently gave encouragement to the other party, which, in 1787, has taken the political field and, with its fashionable dependants and the tongue and the pen, is endeavouring to establish in great haste, a politer kind of government. These two parties, which will probably be opposed or united as it may suit their interests and views, are really insignificant compared with the solid, free and independent part of the community. It is not my intention to suggest that either of these parties and the real friends of the proposed constitution are the same men. The fact is, these aristocrats support and hasten the adoption of the proposed constitution merely because they think it is a stepping stone to their favorite object. I think I am well-founded in this idea; I think the general politics of these men support it, as well as the common observation among them, That the proffered plan is the best that can be got at present; it will do for a few years and lead to something better.

True Patriots Will Not Hurry the Adoption

The sensible and judicious part of the community will carefully weigh all these circumstances; they will view the late convention as a respectable assembly of men—America probably never will see an assembly of men, of a like number, more respectable. But the members of the convention met without knowing the sentiments of one man in ten thousand in these states respecting the new ground taken. Their doings are but the first attempts in the most important scene ever opened. Though each individual in the state conventions will not, probably, be so respectable as each individual in the federal convention, yet as the state conventions will probably consist of fifteen hundred or two thousand men of abilities and versed in the science of government, collected from all parts of the community and from all orders of men, it must be acknowledged that the weight of respectability will be in them. In them will be collected the solid sense and the real political character of the country. Being revisers of the subject, they will possess peculiar advantages. To say that these conventions ought not to attempt, coolly and deliberately, the revision of the system or that they cannot amend it is very foolish or very assuming. If these conventions, after examining the system, adopt it, I shall be perfectly satisfied and wish to see men make the administration of the government an equal blessing to all orders of men. I believe the great body of our people to be virtuous and friendly to good government, to the protection of liberty and property. It is the duty of all good men, especially of those who are placed as sentinels to guard their rights—it is their duty to examine into the prevailing politics of parties and to disclose them—while they avoid exciting undue suspicions, to lay facts before the people, which will enable them to form a proper judgment. Men who wish the people of this country to determine for themselves, and deliberately to fit the government to their situation, must feel some degree of indignation at those attempts to hurry the adoption of a system and to shut the door against examination. The very attempts create suspicions that those who make them have secret views or see some defects in the system, which, in the hurry of affairs, they expect will escape the eye of a free people.

A Time for Careful Examination

What can be the views of those gentlemen in Pennsylvania, who precipitated decisions on this subject? What can be the views of those gentlemen in Boston, who countenanced the printers in shutting up the press against a fair and free investigation of this important system in the usual way? The members of the convention have done their duty. Why should some of them fly to their states—almost forget a propriety of behavior and precipitate measures for the adoption of a system of their own making? I confess candidly, when I consider these circumstances in connection with the unguarded parts of the system I have mentioned, I feel disposed to proceed with very great caution and to pay more attention than usual to the conduct of particular characters. If the constitution presented be a good one, it will stand the test with a well informed people. All are agreed there shall be state conventions to examine it; and we must believe it will be adopted, unless we suppose it is a bad one, or that those conventions will make false divisions respecting it. I admit improper measures are taken against the adoption of the system as well for it. All who object to the plan proposed ought to point out the defects objected to and to propose those amendments with which they can accept it, or to propose some other system of government, that the public mind may be known, and that we may be brought to agree in some system of government, to strengthen and execute the present, or to provide a substitute. I consider the field of inquiry just opened, and that we are to look to the state conventions for ultimate decisions on the subject before us; it is not to be presumed that they will differ about small amendments and lose a system when they shall have made it substantially good; but, touching the essential amendments, it is to be presumed the several conventions will pursue the most rational measures to agree in and obtain them; and such defects as they shall discover and not remove, they will probably notice, keep them in view as the ground work of future amendments, and in the firm and manly language which every free people ought to use, will suggest to those who may hereafter administer the government, that it is their expectation, that the system will be so organized by legislative acts, and the government so administered as to render those defects as little injurious as possible. Our coun-

Antifederalism Is Not Simply the Opposite of Federalism

Political scientists Wilson Carey McWilliams, of Rutgers University and Michael T. Gibbons, of the University of South Florida, argue that the Antifederalists had their own distinct vision of politics. They were not, the authors argue, simply opposed to the U.S. Constitution.

The Founding of the American republic was an extraordinary event. It involved the establishment of a new state by deliberation, not only in the Constitutional Convention but in the searching and prolonged public debate over ratification. . . .

Our understanding of the Founding period has . . . been weakened by our tendency to slight the Antifederalist opponents of the Constitution. Antifederalists included serious political thinkers who were *for* a different sort of regime and not merely opposed to the Constitution. In many respects the debate between the Federalists and Antifederalists involves the great dialogue between ancient and modern theory. But it also includes a debate about the nature of modern representative democracy. The Antifederalists must be included among the Founders not only because of the positive contribution they made to the constitutional debates but because

trymen are entitled to an honest and faithful government; to a government of laws and not of men; and also to one of their choosing. As a citizen of the country, I wish to see these objects secured, and licentious, assuming and overbearing men restrained. If the constitution or social compact be vague and unguarded, then we depend wholly upon the prudence, wisdom and moderation of those who manage the affairs of government; or on what, probably, is equally uncertain and precarious, the success of the people oppressed by the abuse of government, in receiving it from the hands of those who abuse it, and placing it in the hands of those who will use it well.

much of Federalist thought was a response to arguments advanced by the Antifederalists. . . .

The first problem with the new Constitution, claimed the Antifederalists, is that it would corrupt the republican character of the American people. The centralization of power, the alleged transformation of the American spirit to a monarchical one, and the antiregionalism of the new document were all evidence of a conspiracy of the few to corrupt the many. . . . According to the Antifederalists, the evidence of the aims of the conspiracy could be found in the fact that the new Constitution embodied antirepublican principles. . . . The republican character of the people was strengthened in the confederacy of the Articles of Confederation. It maintained rough equality, discouraged luxury, and constrained the pursuit of wealth. These qualities were necessary according to . . . the Antifederalists for genuine liberty. But they were imperiled by a government which the Antifederalists perceived as encouraging commerce, ambition and the pursuit of wealth. The latter required a strong centralized government to control them. A strong centralized government was the antithesis of what the Antifederalists understood as a republic.

Wilson Carey McWilliams and Michael T. Gibbons, "Introduction," *The Federalists, the Antifederalists, and the American Political Tradition.* New York: Greenwood Press, 1992, pp. 2–3.

One Rational Mode of Proceeding

In every point of view, therefore, in which I have been able, as yet, to contemplate this subject, I can discern but one rational mode of proceeding relative to it: and that is to examine it with freedom and candor, to have state conventions some months hence, which shall examine cooly every article, clause, and word in the system proposed and to adopt it with such amendments as they shall think fit. How far the state conventions ought to pursue the mode prescribed by the federal convention of adopting or rejecting the plan in toto, I leave it to them to determine. Our examination of the subject hitherto has been rather of a general nature. The republican characters in the several states, who wish to make this plan more adequate to security of liberty and property, and to the duration of the principles of a free government, will, no doubt, collect their opinions to certain points and accurately define those alterations and amendments they wish. If it shall be found they essentially disagree in them, the conventions will then be able to determine whether to adopt the plan as it is or what will be proper to be done.

Under these impressions, and keeping in view the improper and unadvisable lodgment of powers in the general government, organized as it at present is, touching internal taxes, armies and militia, the elections of its own members, causes between citizens of different states, &c. and the want of a more perfect bill of rights, &c. I drop the subject for the present. When I shall have leisure to revise and correct my ideas respecting it and to collect into points the opinions of those who wish to make the system more secure and safe, perhaps I may proceed to point out particularly for your consideration the amendments which ought to be ingrafted into this system, not only in conformity to my own, but the deliberate opinions of others—you will with me perceive that the objections to the plan proposed may, by a more leisure examination, be set in a stronger point of view, especially the important one, that there is no substantial representation of the people provided for in a government in which the most essential powers, even as to the internal police of the country, is proposed to be lodged.

I think the honest and substantial part of the community will wish to see this system altered [and have] permanency and consistency given to the constitution we shall adopt; and, therefore, they will be anxious to apportion the powers to the features and organization of the government and to see abuse in the exercise of power more effectually guarded against. It is suggested that state officers, . . . [for self-interested] motives, will oppose the constitution presented. I see no reason for this; their places in general will not be affected, but new openings to offices and places of profit must evidently be made by the adoption of the constitution in its present form.

Yours, &c

The FEDERAL FARMER

To the REPUBLICAN

A Federalist Defense

Publius

> Alexander Hamilton, John Jay, and James Madison together
> anonymously wrote a series of eighty-five different letters
> from October 27, 1787, until August 16, 1788, principally
> to persuade New York to ratify the U.S. Constitution. The
> letters were also published together in two separate volumes
> in 1788. These letters, collectively called *The Federalist
> Papers,* are works of political persuasion. They are also theo-
> retical observations about the general nature of society and
> government. In one of the most famous of the letters, *Feder-
> alist No. 51,* James Madison exhibits both aspects. In terms
> of political persuasion, Madison attempts to convince his
> New York audience that separation of powers, checks and
> balances, and federalism, which are embedded in the U.S.
> Constitution, make the U.S. government better. His contribu-
> tion to political theory stems from his observation that politi-
> cians are human and, thus, subject to the human frailties of
> greed and ambition. Madison argues that effective govern-
> ment must walk a tightrope between giving the government
> enough power to rule but at the same time not giving it too
> much power so as to allow ambitious politicians to abuse
> that government.

To the People of the State of New York:
  To WHAT expedient, then, shall we finally resort, for
maintaining in practice the necessary partition of power

From *The Federalist Papers,* by Alexander Hamilton, James Madison, and John Jay, no.
51, 1788.

among the several departments, as laid down in the Constitution? The only answer that can be given is, that as all these exterior provisions are found to be inadequate, the defect must be supplied, by so contriving the interior structure of the government as that its several constituent parts may, by their mutual relations, be the means of keeping each other in their proper places. Without presuming to undertake a full development of this important idea, I will hazard a few general observations, which may perhaps place it in a clearer light, and enable us to form a more correct judgment of the principles and structure of the government planned by the convention.

Separation of Powers

In order to lay a due foundation for that separate and distinct exercise of the different powers of government, which to a certain extent is admitted on all hands to be essential to the preservation of liberty, it is evident that each department should have a will of its own; and consequently should be so constituted that the members of each should have as little agency as possible in the appointment of the members of the others. Were this principle rigorously adhered to, it would require that all the appointments for the supreme executive, legislative, and judiciary magistracies should be drawn from the same fountain of authority, the people, through channels having no communication whatever with one another. Perhaps such a plan of constructing the several departments would be less difficult in practice than it may in contemplation appear. Some difficulties, however, and some additional expense would attend the execution of it. Some deviations, therefore, from the principle must be admitted. In the constitution of the judiciary department in particular, it might be inexpedient to insist rigorously on the principle: first, because peculiar qualifications being essential in the members, the primary consideration ought to be to select that mode of choice which best secures these qualifications; secondly, because the permanent tenure by which the appointments are held in that department, must soon destroy all sense of dependence on the authority conferring them.

It is equally evident, that the members of each department should be as little dependent as possible on those of the others, for the emoluments annexed to their offices. Were the executive magistrate, or the judges, not independent of the legislature in this particular, their independence in every other would be merely nominal.

Checks and Balances

But the great security against a gradual concentration of the several powers in the same department, consists in giving to those who administer each department the necessary constitutional means and personal motives to resist encroachments of the others. The provision for defense must in this, as in all other cases, be made commensurate to the danger of attack. Ambition must be made to counteract ambition. The interest of the man must be connected with the constitutional rights of the place. It may be a reflection on human nature, that such devices should be necessary to control the abuses of government. But what is government itself, but the greatest of all reflections on human nature? If men were angels, no government would be necessary. If angels were to govern men, neither external nor internal controls on government would be necessary. In framing a government which is to be administered by men over men, the great difficulty lies in this: you must first enable the government to control the governed; and in the next place oblige it to control itself. A dependence on the people is, no doubt, the primary control on the government; but experience has taught mankind the necessity of auxiliary precautions.

This policy of supplying, by opposite and rival interests, the defect of better motives, might be traced through the whole system of human affairs, private as well as public. We see it particularly displayed in all the subordinate distributions of power, where the constant aim is to divide and arrange the several offices in such a manner as that each may be a check on the other—that the private interest of every individual may be a sentinel over the public rights. These inventions of prudence cannot be less requisite in the distribution of the supreme powers of the State.

But it is not possible to give to each department an equal power of self-defense. In republican government, the legislative authority necessarily predominates. The remedy for this inconveniency is to divide the legislature into different branches; and to render them, by different modes of election and different principles of action, as little connected with each other as the nature of their common functions and their common dependence on the society will admit. It may even be necessary to guard against dangerous encroachments by still further precautions. As the weight of the legislative authority requires that it should be thus divided, the weakness of the executive may require, on the other hand, that it should be fortified. An absolute negative on the legislature appears, at first view, to be the natural defence with which the executive magistrate should be armed. But perhaps it would be neither altogether safe nor alone sufficient. On ordinary occasions it might not be exerted with the requisite firmness, and on extraordinary occasions it might be perfidiously abused. May not this defect of an absolute negative be supplied by some qualified connection between this weaker department and the weaker branch of the stronger department, by which the latter may be led to support the constitutional rights of the former, without being too much detached from the rights of its own department?

If the principles on which these observations are founded be just, as I persuade myself they are, and they be applied as a criterion to the several state constitutions, and to the federal Constitution, it will be found that if the latter does not perfectly correspond with them, the former are infinitely less able to bear such a test.

There are, moreover, two considerations particularly applicable to the federal system of America, which place that system in a very interesting point of view.

First. In a single republic, all the power surrendered by the people is submitted to the administration of a single government; and the usurpations are guarded against by a division of the government into distinct and separate departments. In the compound republic of America, the power surrendered by the people is first divided between two distinct governments, and then the portion allotted to each subdivided among distinct and separate departments. Hence a double security arises to the rights of the people. The different governments will control each other, at the same time that each will be controlled by itself.

Second. It is of great importance in a republic not only to guard the society against the oppression of its rulers, but to guard one part of the society against the injustice of the other part. Different interests necessarily exist in different classes of citizens. If a majority be united by a common interest, the rights of the minority will be insecure. There are but two methods of providing against this evil: the one by creating a will in the community independent of the majority—that is, of the society itself; the other, by comprehending in the society so many separate descriptions of citizens as will render an unjust combination of a majority of the whole very improbable, if not impracticable. The first method prevails in all governments possessing a hereditary or self-appointed authority. This, at best, is but a precarious security; because a power independent of the society may as well espouse the unjust views of the major, as the rightful interests of the minor party, and may possibly be turned against both parties. The second method will be exemplified in the federal republic of the United States. Whilst all authority in it will be derived from and dependent on the society, the society itself will be broken into so many parts, interests, and in the other in the multiplicity of sects. The degree of security in both cases will depend on the number of interests and classes of citizens, that the rights of individuals, or of the minority, will be in little danger from interested combinations of the majority. In a free government the security for civil rights must be the same as that for religious rights. It consists in the one case in the multiplicity of interests, and in the other in the multiplicity of sects. The degree of security in both cases will depend on the number of interests and sects and this may be presumed to depend on the extent of country and number of people comprehended under the same government. This view of the subject must particularly recommend a proper federal system to all the sincere and considerate friends of republican government, since it shows that in exact proportion as the territory of the Union may be formed into more circumscribed Confederacies, or states, oppressive combinations of a majority will be facilitated; the best security, under the republican forms, for the rights of every class of citizens, will be diminished; and consequently the stability and independence of some member of the government, the only other security, must be proportionally increased.

Supporting a Strong Government Is in Everybody's Best Interest

Justice is the end of government. It is the end of civil society. It ever has been and ever will be pursued until it be obtained, or until liberty be lost in the pursuit. In a society under the forms of which the stronger faction can readily unite and oppress the weaker, anarchy may as truly be said to reign as in a state of nature, where the weaker individual is not secured against the violence of the stronger; and as, in the latter state, even the stronger individuals are prompted, by the uncertainty of their condition, to submit to a government which may protect the weak as well as themselves; so, in the former state, will the more powerful factions or parties be gradually induced, by a like motive, to wish for a government which will protect all parties, the weaker as well as the more powerful. It can be little doubted that if the state of Rhode Island was separated from the Confederacy and left to itself, the insecurity of rights under the popular form of government within such narrow limits would be displayed by such reiterated oppressions of factious majorities that some power altogether independent of the people would soon be called for by the voice of the very factions whose misrule had proved the necessity of it. In the extended republic of the United States, and among the great variety of interests, parties, and sects which it embraces, a coalition of a majority of the whole society could seldom take place on any other principles than those of justice and the general good; whilst there being thus less danger to a minor from the will of a major party, there must be less pretext, also, to provide for the security of the former, by introducing into the government a will not dependent on the latter, or, in other words, a will independent of the society itself. It is no less certain than it is important, notwithstanding the contrary opinions which have been entertained, that the larger the society, provided it lie within a practical sphere, the more duly capable it will be of self-government. And happily for the *republican cause,* the practicable sphere may be carried to a very great extent, by a judicious modification and mixture of the *federal principle.*

PUBLIUS

Chapter 5

The Ratification Debate and the Bill of Rights

Chapter Preface

Each state's ratifying convention had its own dynamic; however, the Massachusetts convention represents one of the most significant and contentious. Its large size and economic strength ensured that Massachusetts was a vital state for America's survival under the Constitution. Additionally, the strategy adopted by the Massachusetts convention provided a blueprint for all subsequent ratifying conventions to incorporate the concerns of the Anti-Federalists without rejecting the Constitution.

At the start of the Massachusetts convention, it seemed the Anti-Federalists would comfortably prevail. Governor John Hancock was the presiding officer of the convention, and he strongly opposed the Constitution. Furthermore, it was estimated that Anti-Federalists outnumbered Federalists by a margin of at least three to one. Since the early seventeenth century Massachusetts, as both a colony and a state, widely relied on town hall meetings, where citizens would directly vote on community matters. The citizens of Massachusetts also prided themselves on yearly elections as a way of holding their elected representatives accountable. This made many Massachusetts delegates reticent to support the Constitution, with its representative democracy and elected officials in office for two, four, and even six years. Additionally, the western counties of Massachusetts sent delegates who simply did not trust any elected body because they vividly remembered Shays's Rebellion and the fact that the Massachusetts Assembly completely ignored their calls for tax relief. In fact, twenty-nine of the delegates had actually fought with Daniel Shays in the rebellion. Finally, Massachusetts history—for example, the Boston Tea Party, the ride of Paul Revere, and the Battles of Concord and Lexington—made many Massachusetts delegates loathe to agree to any document without explicit protections for individual rights.

Supporters of the Constitution had to act carefully to convince the Massachusetts convention to ratify the Constitution. Throughout the debates, the Federalists were unfailingly respectful of the Anti-Federalists and carefully listened to what they said. Supporters also knew that Massachusetts would not ratify the Constitution unless Hancock agreed. Samuel Adams, the instigator of the Boston Tea Party and a good friend of Hancock, favored ratification of the Constitution. Convincing Hancock was not simply a matter of Adams asking an old friend for a favor. Therefore, Adams and the other Federalists also adopted an ingenious strategy. If the Anti-Federalists agreed to vote in favor of the Constitution, the Federalists would agree to submit with their ratification decree a list of possible amendments to the Constitution to reflect the primary concerns of the Anti-Federalists. They decided that Hancock must be the one to make this suggestion to the convention. To convince the vain Hancock, they suggested that he would probably be elected the first president of the United States if he could get the Massachusetts convention to ratify the Constitution.

The next day Hancock presented to the Massachusetts convention the Hancock Proposition. Hancock suggested that Massachusetts should ratify the Constitution but also provide a list of amendments that it would like to see adopted. Even with this, Massachusetts barely ratified the Constitution, by a majority of only 19 votes out of 355 cast. However, many states that still had not ratified the Constitution—including New York and Virginia—now had a strategy that would convince moderate Anti-Federalists to ratify the Constitution.

A Passionate Call for Ratification

Alexander Hamilton

New York, one of the most important states due to its size and commercial wealth, was closely divided over whether to ratify the U.S. Constitution. Alexander Hamilton was a delegate to the Constitutional Convention and to the New York state ratification convention. As one of the co-authors of *The Federalist Papers* and a prominent New York politician, Hamilton was a strong supporter of the Constitution. On Friday, June 20, and Saturday June 21, 1788, Alexander Hamilton explained to the New York ratification convention his reasons for supporting the U.S. Constitution. New York eventually ratified the Constitution by a very narrow margin, 30–27.

[M]r. Chairman] Let us consider the Constitution calmly and dispassionately, and attend to those things only which merit consideration.

No arguments drawn from embarrassment or inconvenience ought to prevail upon us to adopt a system of government radically bad; yet it is proper that these arguments, among others, should be brought into view. In doing this, yesterday, it was necessary to reflect upon our situation, to dwell upon the imbecility of our union and to consider whether we, as a state, could stand alone. Although I am persuaded this Convention will be resolved to adopt nothing that is bad, yet I think every prudent man will consider the merits of the plan

Reprinted from *The Debates in the Several State Conventions on the Adoption of the Federal Constitution, as Recommended by the General Convention at Philadelphia in 1787,* vol. 2, collected by Jonathan Elliot (Washington, DC, 1836–1845).

in connection with the circumstances of our country, and that a rejection of the Constitution may involve most fatal consequences. I make these remarks to show that, though we ought not to be actuated by unreasonable fear, yet we ought to be prudent. . . .

No Use in Correcting the Old Articles

Sir, it appears to me extraordinary, that, while gentlemen in one breath acknowledge that the old Confederation requires many material amendments, they should in the next deny that its defects have been the cause of our political weakness, and the consequent calamities of our country. I cannot but infer from this, that there is still some lurking favorite imagination, that this system, with correctness, might become a safe and permanent one. It is proper that we should examine this matter. We contend that the radical vice in the old Confederation is, that the laws of the Union apply only to states in their corporate capacity. Has not every man who has been in our legislature experienced the truth of this position? It is inseparable from the disposition of bodies, who have a constitutional power of resistance, to examine the merits of a law. This has ever been the case with the federal requisitions. In this examination, not being furnished with those lights which directed the deliberations of the general government, and incapable of embracing the general interests of the Union, the states have almost uniformly weighed the requisitions by their own local interests, and have only executed them so far as answered their particular convenience or advantage. Hence there have ever been thirteen different bodies to judge of the measures of Congress, and the operations of government have been distracted by their taking different courses. Those which were to be benefited have complied with the requisitions; other have totally disregarded them. Have not all of us been witnesses to the unhappy embarrassments which resulted from these proceedings? Even during the late war, while the pressure of common danger connected strongly the bond of our union, and incited to vigorous exertion, we have felt many distressing effects of the important system. How have we seen this state, though most exposed to the calamities of the war, complying, in an unexampled manner, with the federal requisitions, and compelled by the delinquency of others to bear most unusual burdens! Of this truth we have the most solemn proof on our records. In 1779 and '80, when the state, from the ravages of war, and from her great exertions to resist them, became weak, distressed and forlorn, every man avowed the principle which we now contend for— that our misfortunes, in a great degree, proceeded from the want of vigor in the Continental government. These were our sentiments when we did not speculate, but feel. We saw our weakness, and found ourselves its victims. Let us reflect that this may again, in all probability, be our situation. This is a weak state, and its relative state is dangerous. Your capital is accessible by land, and by sea is exposed to every daring invader; and on the north-west you are open to the inroads of a powerful foreign nation. Indeed, this state, from its situation, will, in time of war, probably be the theatre of its operations.

A Nation at War with Itself

Gentlemen have said that the non-compliance of the states had been occasioned by their sufferings. This may in part be true. But has this state been delinquent? Amidst all our distresses, *we* have fully complied. If New York could comply wholly with the requisitions, is it not to be supposed that the other states could in part comply? Certainly every state in the Union might have executed them in some degree. But New Hampshire, which has not suffered at all, is totally delinquent. North Carolina is totally delinquent. Many others have contributed in a very small proportion. And Pennsylvania and New York are the only states which have perfectly discharged their federal duty.

From the delinquency of those states which have suffered little by the war, we naturally conclude, that they have made no efforts; and a knowledge of human nature will teach us that their ease and security have been a principal cause of their want of exertion. While danger is distant, its impression is weak; and while it affects only our neighbors, we have few

motives to provide against it. Sir, if we have national objects
to pursue, we must have national revenues. If you make requisitions, and they are not complied with, what is to be done?
It has been observed, to coerce the states is one of the mad-
dest projects that was ever devised. A failure of compliance
will never be confined to a single state. This being the case,
can we suppose it wise to hazard a civil war? Suppose Massachusetts, or any large state, should refuse, and Congress
should attempt to compel them, would they not have influence to procure assistance, especially from those states which
are in the same situation as themselves? What picture does
this idea present to our view? A complying state at war with
a non-complying state; Congress marching the troops of one
state into the bosom of another; this state collecting auxil-
iaries, and forming, perhaps, a majority against its federal
head. Here is a nation at war with itself. Can any reasonable
man be well disposed towards a government which makes
war and carnage the only means of supporting itself—a
government that can exist only by the sword? Every such war
must involve the innocent with the guilty. This single consideration should be sufficient to dispose every peaceable citizen against such a government. . . .

The Need for a Totally Different Government

What, then, shall we do? Shall we take the old Confederation, as the basis of a new system? Can this be the object of
the gentlemen? Certainly not. Will any man, who entertains
a wish for the safety of his country, trust the sword and the
purse with a single assembly organized on principles so defective—so rotten? Though we might give to such a government certain powers with safety, yet to give them the full and
unlimited powers of taxation and the national forces, would
be to establish a despotism; the definition of which is, a government in which all power is concentrated in a single body.
To take the old Confederation, and fashion it upon these principles, would be establishing a power which would destroy
the liberties of the people. These considerations show clearly

that a government totally different must be instituted. They had weight in the Convention who formed the new system. It was seen that the necessary powers were too great to be trusted to a single body; they therefore formed two branches, and divided the powers, that each might be check upon the other. This was the result of their wisdom; and I presume that every reasonable man will agree to it. The more this subject is explained, the more clear and convincing it will appear to every member of this body. The fundamental principle of the old Confederation is defective; we must totally eradicate and discard this principle before we can expect an efficient government. The gentlemen who have spoken to-day have taken up the subject of the ancient confederacies; but their view of them has been extremely partial and erroneous. The fact is, the same false and impracticable principle ran through the ancient governments. . . .

We shall do well, sir, not to deceive ourselves with the favorable events of the late war. Common danger prevented the operation of the ruinous principle, in its full extent, but, since the peace, we have experienced the evils; we have felt the poison of the system in its unmingled purity. . . .

Principles of the Convention

In order that the committee may understand clearly the principles on which the general Convention acted, I think it necessary to explain some preliminary circumstances. Sir, the natural situation of this country seems to divide its interests into different classes. There are navigating and non-navigating states. The Northern are properly navigating states; the Southern appear to possess neither the means nor the spirit of navigation. This difference of situation naturally produces a dissimilarity of interests and views respecting foreign commerce. It was the interest of the Northern States that there should be no restraints on their navigation, and they should have full power, by a majority in Congress, to make commercial regulations in favor of their own, and in restraint of the navigation of foreigners. The Southern States wish to impose a restraint on the Northern, by requiring that two-thirds in Congress should be requisite to pass an act in regulation of commerce. They were apprehensive that the restraints of a navigation law would discourage foreigners, and, by obliging them to employ the shipping of the Northern States, would probably enhance their freight. This being the case, they insisted strenuously on having this provision ingrafted in the Constitution, and the Northern States were as anxious in opposing it. On the other hand, the small states, seeing themselves embraced by the Confederation upon equal terms, wished to retain the advantages which they already possessed. The large states, on the contrary, thought it improper that Rhode Island and Delaware should enjoy an equal suffrage with themselves. From these sources a delicate and difficult contest arose. It become necessary, therefore, to compromise, or the Convention must have dissolved without effecting any thing. Would it have been wise and prudent in that body, in this critical situation, to have deserted their country? No. Every man who hears me, every wise man in the United States, would have condemned them. The Convention was obliged to appoint a committee for accommodation. In this committee, the arrangement was formed as it now stands, and their report was accepted. It was a delicate point, and it was necessary that all parties should be indulged. Gentlemen will see that, if there had not been a unanimity, nothing could have been done; for the Convention had no power to establish, but only to recommend, a government. Any other system would have been impracticable. Let a convention be called tomorrow; let them meet twenty times—nay, twenty thousand times—they will have the same difficulties to encounter, the same clashing interests to reconcile. . . .

Slavery and Representation

The first thing objected to is that clause which allows a representation for three-fifths of the *negroes*. Much has been said of the impropriety of representing men who have no will of their own. Whether this be reasoning or declamation, I will not presume to say. It is the unfortunate situation of the

Southern States to have a great part of their population, as well as property, in blacks. The regulation complained of was one result of the spirit of accommodation which governed the Convention, and without this indulgence no union could possibly have been formed. But, sir, considering some peculiar advantages which we derive from them, it is entirely just that they should be gratified. The Southern States possess certain staples,—tobacco, rice, indigo, &c.,—which must be capital objects in treaties of commerce with foreign nations; and the advantages which they necessarily procure in those treaties will be felt throughout all the states. But the justice of this plan will appear in another view. The best writers on government have held that representation should be compounded of persons and property. This rule has been adopted, as far as it could be, in the constitution of New York. It will, however, by no means be admitted that the slaves are considered altogether as property. They are men, though degraded to the condition of slavery. They are persons known to the municipal laws of the states which they inhabit, as well as to the laws of nature. But representation and taxation go together, and one uniform rule ought to apply to both. Would it be just to compute these slaves in the assessment of taxes, and discard them from the estimate in the apportionment of representatives? Would it be just to impose a singular burden, without conferring some adequate advantage? . . .

Sir, we hear constantly a great deal which is rather calculated to awake our passions, and create prejudices, than to conduct us to the truth, and teach us our real interests. I do not suppose this to be the design of the gentlemen. Why, then, are we told so often of an aristocracy? For my part, I hardly know the meaning of this word as it is applied. If all we hear be true, this government is really a very bad one. But who are the aristocracy among us? Where do we find men elevated to a perpetual rank above their fellow citizens, and possessing powers entirely independent of them? The arguments of the gentlemen only go to prove that there are men who are rich, men who are poor, some who are wise, and others who are not; that, indeed, every distinguished man is an aristocrat.

This reminds me of a description of the aristocrats I have seen in a late publication styled the Federal Farmer [*Letters from the Federal Farmer to the Republican*]. The author reckons in the aristocracy all governors of states, members of Congress, chief magistrates and all officers of the militia. This description, I presume to say, is ridiculous. The image is a phantom. Does the new government render a rich man more eligible than a poor one? No. It requires no such qualification. It is bottomed on the broad and equal principle of your state constitution. . . .

Sir, if the people have it in their option to elect their most meritorious men, is this to be considered as an objection? Shall the Constitution oppose their wishes and abridge their most invaluable privilege? While property continues to be pretty equally divided and a considerable share of information pervades the community, the tendency of the people's suffrages will be to elevate merit even from obscurity. As riches increase and accumulate in few hands, as luxury prevails in society, virtue will be in a greater degree considered as only a graceful appendage of wealth, and the tendency of things will be to depart from the republican standard. This is the real disposition of human nature: it is what neither the honorable member nor myself can correct; it is a common misfortune, that awaits our state constitution as well as all others.

There is an advantage incident to large districts of election, which perhaps the gentlemen, amidst all their apprehensions of influence and bribery, have not adverted to. In large districts, the corruption of the electors is much more difficult; combinations for the purposes of intrigue are less easily formed; factions and cabals are little known. In a small district, wealth will have a more complete influence, because the people in the vicinity of a great man are more immediately his dependants, and because this influence has fewer objects to act upon. It has been remarked, that it would be disagreeable to the middle class of men to go to the seat of the new government. If this be so, the difficulty will be enhanced by the gentleman's proposal. If his argument be true, it proves that the larger the representation is, the less will be your chance of having it filled. But it appears to me frivolous to bring forward such arguments as these. It has answered no other purpose than to induce me, by way of reply, to enter into discussion, which I consider as useless, and not applicable to our subject.

It is a harsh doctrine that men grow wicked in proportion as they improve and enlighten their minds. Experience has by no means justified us in the supposition that there is more virtue in one class of men than in another. Look through the rich and the poor of the community, the learned and the ignorant. Where does virtue predominate? The difference indeed consists, not in the quantity, but kind, of vices which are incident to various classes; and here the advantage of character belongs to the wealthy. Their vices are probably more favorable to the prosperity of the state than those of the indigent, and partake less of moral depravity.

After all, sir, we must submit to this idea, that the true principle of a republic is, that the people should choose whom they please to govern them. Representation is imperfect in proportion as the current of popular favor is checked. This great source of free government, popular election, should be perfectly pure, and the most unbounded liberty allowed. Where this principle is adhered to; where, in the organization of the government, the legislative, executive, and judicial branches are rendered distinct; where, again, the legislature is divided into separate houses, and the operations of each are controlled by various checks and balances, and, above all, by the vigilance and weight of the state governments—to talk of tyranny, and the subversion of our liberties, is to speak the language of enthusiasm. This balance between the national and state governments ought to be dwelt on with peculiar attention, as it is of the utmost importance. It forms a double security to the people. If one encroaches on their rights, they will find a powerful protection in the other. Indeed, they will both be prevented from overpassing their constitutional limits, by a certain rivalship, which will ever subsist between them. I am persuaded that a firm union is as necessary to perpetuate our liberties as it is to make us respectable, and experience will probably prove that the national government will be as natural a guardian of our freedom as the state legislature themselves.

Rectifying the People's Unhappy Situation

Suggestions, sir, of an extraordinary nature, have been frequently thrown out in the course of the present political controversy. It gives me pain to dwell on topics of this kind, and I wish they might be dismissed. We have been told that the old Confederation has proved inefficacious only because intriguing and powerful men, aiming at a revolution, have been forever instigating the people, and rendering them disaffected with it. This, sir, is a false insinuation. The thing is impossible. I will venture to assert, that no combination of designing men under heaven will be capable of making a government unpopular which is in its principles a wise and good one, and vigorous in its operations.

The Confederation was framed amidst the agitation and tumults of society. It was composed of unsound materials, put together in haste. Men of intelligence discovered the feebleness of the structure, in the first stages of its existence; but the great body of the people, too much engrossed with their distresses to contemplate any but the immediate causes of them, were ignorant of the defects of their constitution. But when the dangers of war were removed, they saw clearly what they had suffered, and what they had yet to suffer, from a feeble form of government. There was no need of discerning men to convince the people of their unhappy situation; the complaint was coextensive with the evil, and both were common to all classes of the community. We have been told that the spirit of patriotism and love of liberty are almost extinguished among the people, and that it has become a prevailing doctrine that republican principles ought to be hooted out of the world. Sir, I am confident that such remarks as these are rather occasioned by the heat of argument than by a cool conviction of their truth and justice. As far as my experience has extended, I have heard no such doctrine; nor have I discovered any diminution of regard for those rights and liberties, in defence of which the people have fought and suffered. There have been, undoubtedly, some men who have had speculative doubts on the subject of government; but the principles of republicanism are founded on too firm a basis to be shaken by a few speculative and skeptical reasoners. Our error has been of a very different kind. We have erred through excess of caution, and a zeal false and impracticable. Our counsels have been destitute of consistency and stability. I am flattered with the hope, sir, that we have now found a cure for the evils under which we have so long labored. I trust that the proposed Constitution affords a genuine specimen of representative and republican government, and that it will answer, in an eminent degree, all the beneficial purposes of society.

A Spirited Attack by a Famous Patriot

Patrick Henry

Patrick Henry, the famous Virginia patriot who argued in favor of American independence from Great Britain by saying, "Give me liberty or give me death!" was not a fan of the U.S. Constitution. He refused appointment to the Constitutional Convention, but he did attend the ratifying convention in Virginia, where his fiery oratory attacked the U.S. Constitution as a threat to individual liberties and states' rights. Nearly one-third of the debate in the Virginia convention was taken by Patrick Henry's criticisms of the U.S. Constitution. These excerpts come from speeches given by Patrick Henry on Wednesday, June 4; Thursday, June 5; Monday, June 23; and Wednesday, June 25, 1788.

Mr. Chairman, the public mind, as well as my own, is extremely uneasy at the proposed change of government. Give me leave to form one of the number of those who wish to be thoroughly acquainted with the reasons of this perilous and uneasy situation, and why we are brought hither to decide on this great national question. I consider myself as the servant of the people of this commonwealth, as a sentinel over their rights, liberty and happiness. I represent their feelings when I say that they are exceedingly uneasy at being brought from that state of full security, which they enjoyed, to the present delusive appearance of things. A year ago, the minds of our citizens were at perfect repose. Before the meeting of the late federal Convention at

Reprinted from *The Debates in the Several State Conventions on the Adoption of the Federal Constitution, as Recommended by the General Convention at Philadelphia in 1787,* vol. 3, collected by Jonathan Elliot (Washington, DC, 1836–1845).

Philadelphia, a general peace and a universal tranquillity prevailed in this country; but, since that period, they are exceedingly uneasy and disquieted. When I wished for an appointment to this Convention, my mind was extremely agitated for the situation of public affairs. I conceived the republic to be in extreme danger. If our situation be thus uneasy, whence has arisen this fearful jeopardy? It arises from this fatal system; it arises from a proposal to change our government—a proposal that goes to the utter annihilation of the must solemn engagements of the states—a proposal of establishing nine states into a confederacy, to the eventual exclusion of four states. It goes to the annihilation of those solemn treaties we have formed with foreign nations.

The present circumstances of France—the good offices rendered us by that kingdom—require our most faithful and most punctual adherence to our treaty with her. We are in alliance with the Spaniards, the Dutch, the Prussians; those treaties bound us as thirteen states confederated together. Yet here is a proposal to sever that confederacy. Is it possible that we shall abandon all our treaties and national engagements?—and for what? I expected to hear the reasons for an event so unexpected to my mind and many others. Was our civil polity, or public justice, endangered or sapped? Was the real existence of the country threatened, or was this preceded by a mournful progression of events? This proposal of altering our federal government is of a most alarming nature! Make the best of this new government—say it is composed by any thing but inspiration—you ought to be extremely cautious, watchful, jealous of your liberty; for, instead of securing your rights, you may lose them forever. If a wrong step be now made, the republic may be lost forever. If this new government will not come up to the expectation of the people and [if] they shall be disappointed, their liberty will be lost, and tyranny must and will arise. I repeat it again, and I beg gentlemen to consider, that a wrong step, made now, will plunge us into misery, and our republic will be lost. It will be necessary for this Convention to have a faithful historical detail of the facts that preceded the session of the federal Convention, and the reasons that actuated its members in proposing an entire alteration of government, and to demonstrate the dangers that awaited us. If they were of such awful magnitude as to warrant a proposal so extremely perilous as this, I must assert, that this Convention has an absolute right to a thorough discovery of every circumstance relative to this great event.

And here I would make this inquiry of those worthy characters who composed a part of the late federal Convention. I am sure they were fully impressed with the necessity of forming a great consolidated government, instead of a confederation. That this is a consolidated government is demonstrably clear; and the danger of such a government is, to my mind, very striking. I have the highest veneration for those gentlemen; but, sir, give me leave to demand, What right had they to say, *We, the people?* My political curiosity, exclusive of my anxious solicitude for the public welfare, leads me to ask, Who authorized them to speak the language of, *We, the people,* instead of, *We, the states?* States are the characteristics and the soul of a confederation. If the states be not the agents of this compact, it must be one great, consolidated, national government, of the people of all the states. I have the highest respect for those gentlemen who formed the Convention, and were some of them not here, I would express some testimonial of esteem for them. America had, on a former occasion, put the utmost confidence in them—a confidence which was well placed; and I am sure, sir, I would give up anything to them; I would cheerfully confide in them as my representatives. But, sir, on this great occasion, I would demand the cause of their conduct. Even from that illustrious man who saved us by his valor [i.e., George Washington], I would have a reason for his conduct: that liberty which he has given us by his valor, tells me to ask this reason; and sure I am, were he here, he would give us that reason. But there are other gentlemen here, who can give us this information. The people gave them no power to use their name. That they exceeded their power is perfectly clear. It is not mere curiosity that actuates me. I wish to hear the real, actual, existing danger, which should lead us to take those steps, so dangerous in my conception. Disorders have arisen in other parts of America; but here, sir, no dangers, no insurrection or tumult have happened; every thing has been calm and tranquil. But, not withstanding this, we are wandering on the great ocean of human affairs. I see no landmark to guide us. We are running we know not whither. Difference of opinion has gone to a degree of inflammatory resentment in different parts of the country which has been occasioned by this perilous innovation. The federal Convention ought to have amended the old system; for this purpose they were solely delegated; the object of their mission extended to no other consideration. You must, therefore, forgive the solicitation of one unworthy member to know what danger could have arisen under the present Confederation, and what are the causes of this proposal to change our government. . . .

Unsecured Liberties

Here is a resolution as radical as that which separated us from Great Britain. It is radical in this transition; our rights and privileges are endangered, and the sovereignty of the states will be relinquished: and cannot we plainly see that this is actually the case? The rights of conscience, trial by jury, liberty of the press, all your immunities and franchises, all pretensions to human rights and privileges are rendered insecure, if not lost, by this change, so loudly talked of by some, and inconsiderately by others. Is this tame relinquishment of rights worthy of freemen? Is it worthy of that manly fortitude that ought to characterize republicans? It is said eight states have adopted this plan. I declare that if twelve states and a half had adopted it, I would, with manly firmness, and in spite of an erring world, reject it. You are not to inquire how your trade may be increased, nor how you are to become a great and powerful people, but how your liberties can be secured; for liberty ought to be the direct end of your government.

Having premised these things, I shall, with the aid of my judgment and information, which, I confess, are not extensive, go into the discussion of this system more minutely. Is it necessary for your liberty that you should abandon those great rights by the adoption of this system? Is the relinquishment of the trial by jury and the liberty of the press necessary for your liberty? Will the abandonment of your most sacred rights tend to the security of your liberty? Liberty, the greatest of all earthly blessings—give us that precious jewel, and you may take every thing else! But I am fearful I have lived long enough to become an old-fashioned fellow. Perhaps an invincible attachment to the dearest rights of man may, in these refined, enlightened days, be deemed old-fashioned; if so, I am contented to be so. I say, the time has been when every pulse of my heart beat for American liberty, and which, I believe, had a counterpart in the breast of every true American; but suspicions have gone forth—suspicions of my integrity—publicly reported that my professions are not real. Twenty-three years ago was I supposed a traitor to my country? I was then said to be the bane of sedition, because I supported the rights of my country. I may be thought suspicious when I say our privileges and rights are in danger. But, sir, a number of the people of this country are weak enough to think these things are too true. I am happy to find that the gentleman on the other side declares they are groundless. But, sir, suspicion is a virtue as long as its object is the preservation of the public good, and as long as it stays within proper bounds. Should it fall on me, I am contented: conscious rectitude is a powerful consolation. I trust there are many who think my professions for the public good to be real. Let your suspicion look to both sides. There are many on the other side, who possibly may have been persuaded to the necessity of these measures, which I conceive to be dangerous to your liberty. Guard with jealous attention the public liberty. Suspect every one who approaches that jewel. Unfortunately, nothing will preserve it but downright force. Whenever you give up that force, you are inevitably ruined. . . .

Consider our situation, sir. Go to the poor man, and ask him what he does. He will inform you that he enjoys the fruits of his labor, under his own fig-tree, with his wife and children around him, in peace and security. Go to every other member of society, [and] you will find the same tranquil ease and content; you will find no alarms or disturbances. Why, then, tell us of danger, to terrify us into an adoption of this new form of government? And yet who knows the dangers that this new system may produce? They are out of the sight of the common people, they cannot foresee latent consequences. I dread the operation of it on the middling and lower classes of people; it is for them I fear the adoption of this system. I fear I tire the patience of the Committee, but I beg to be indulged with a few more observations. When I thus profess myself an advocate for the liberty of the people, I shall be told I am a designing man, that I am to be a great man, that I am to be a demagogue and many similar illiberal insinuations will be thrown out. But, Sir, conscious rectitude outweighs those things with me. I see great jeopardy in this new government. I see none from our present one. I hope some gentleman or other will bring forth, in full array, those dangers, if there be any, that we may see and touch them. I have said that I thought this a consolidated government; I will now prove it. Will the great rights of the people be secured by this government? Suppose it should prove oppressive, how can it be altered? Our bill of rights declares, "that a majority of the community hath an indubitable, inalienable, and indefeasible right to reform, alter, or abolish it, in such manner as shall be judged most conducive to the public weal." . . .

This Constitution is said to have beautiful features; but when I come to examine these features, sir, they appear to me horribly frightful. Among other deformities, it has an awful squinting; it squints towards monarchy; and does not this raise indignation in the breast of every true American?

Your President may easily become king. Your Senate is so imperfectly constructed that your dearest rights may be sacrificed by what may be a small minority; and a very small minority may continue forever unchangeably this government, although horridly defective. Where are your checks

in this government? Your strongholds will be in the hands
of your enemies. It is on a supposition that your American
governors shall be honest, that all the good qualities of this
government are founded; but its defective and imperfect
construction puts it in their power to perpetrate the worst of
mischiefs, should they be bad men. And, Sir, would not all
the world, from the eastern to the western hemisphere,
blame our distracted folly in resting our rights upon the con-
tingency of our rulers being good or bad? Show me that age
and country where the rights and liberties of the people were
placed on the sole chance of their rulers being good men,
without a consequent loss of liberty! I say that the loss of
that dearest privilege has ever followed, with absolute certainty, every such mad attempt.

If your American chief be a man of ambition and abilities,
how easy is it for him to render himself absolute! The army
is in his hands, and if he be a man of address, it will be attached to him, and it will be the subject of long meditation
with him to seize the first auspicious moment to accomplish
his design. And, sir, will the American spirit solely relieve
you when this happens? I would rather infinitely—and I am
sure most of this Convention are of the same opinion—have
a king, lords, and commons, than a government so replete
with such insupportable evils. If we make a king, we may
prescribe the rules by which he shall rule his people, and in-
terpose such checks as shall prevent him from infringing
them; but the President, in the field, at the head of his army,
can prescribe the terms on which he shall reign master, so far
that it will puzzle any American ever to get his neck from under the galling yoke. I cannot with patience think of this idea.
If ever he violates the laws, one of two things will happen:
he will come at the head of his army, to carry every thing before him; or he will give bail, or do what Mr. Chief Justice
will order him. If he be guilty, will not the recollection of his
crimes teach him to make one bold push for the American
throne? Will not the immense difference between being master of every thing, and being ignominiously tried and punished, powerfully excite him to make this bold push? But, sir,

where is the existing force to punish him? Can he not, at the head of his army, beat down every opposition? Away with your President! We shall have a king. The army will salute him monarch. Your militia will leave you and assist in making him king and fight against you. And what have you to oppose this force? What will then become of you and your rights? Will not absolute despotism ensue? . . .

The manner in which the judiciary and other branches of the government are formed, seems to me calculated to lay prostrate the states and the liberties of the people. But, Sir, another circumstance ought totally to reject that plan, in my opinion; which is, that it cannot be understood, in many parts, even by the supporters of it. A constitution, sir, ought to be, like a beacon, held up to the public eye so as to be understood by every man. Some gentlemen have observed that the word *jury* implies a jury of the vicinage [vicinity, neighborhood]. There are so many inconsistencies in this, that, for my part, I cannot understand it. By the bill of rights of England, a subject has a right to a trial by his peers. What is meant by his peers? Those who reside near him, his neighbors, and who are well acquainted with his character and situation in life. Is this secured in the proposed plan before you? No, sir. . . .

I beg pardon of this house for having taken up more time than came to my share, and I thank them for the patience and polite attention with which I have been heard. If I shall be in the minority, I shall have those painful sensations which arise from a conviction of *being overpowered in a good cause.* Yet I will be a peaceable citizen. My head, my hand, and my heart shall be at liberty to retrieve the loss of liberty, and remove the defects of that system in a constitutional way. I wish not to go to violence but will wait with hopes that the spirit which predominated in the revolution is not yet gone, nor the cause of those who are attached to the revolution yet lost. I shall, therefore, patiently wait in expectation of seeing that government changed, so as to be compatible with the safety, liberty and happiness, of the people.

The Ratification Compromise: Ratify with Amendments

Delegates to the Massachusetts Ratifying Convention

The U.S. Constitution was forged on several important compromises: the Great Compromise, which created a bicameral legislature with one house apportioned by population and the other having equal representation for all states, and the Three-Fifths Compromise, which allowed slaves to be counted as three-fifths of a person for representation and tax purposes only. One further compromise was needed in the ratification stage. Many individuals were concerned that certain rights and liberties were not expressly protected in the Constitution. They began demanding that a bill of rights be added to the Constitution before they would agree to ratify it. As the Constitution Convention had already completed its work—and it was unlikely that a new convention would be feasible or as successful as the 1787 Convention—many states ratified the Constitution on the provision that a bill of rights would be added as amendments to the Constitution.

One such state was Massachusetts, which served as a model for other states who had reservations about certain aspects of the Constitution. The president of the Massachusetts Ratifying Convention was John Hancock, the prominent signer of the Declaration of Independence. He proposed that Massachusetts should accept the Constitution only with the explicit proviso that it wished to see a bill of rights added to the document. The debates that ensued from his suggestion, coupled with

Reprinted from *The Debates in the Several State Conventions on the Adoption of the Federal Constitution, as Recommended by the General Convention at Philadelphia in 1787,* vol. 2, collected by Jonathan Elliot (Washington, DC, 1836–1845).

the close vote (187-168) by which Massachusetts ratified the Constitution with amendments, suggest that an addition of a bill of rights was a necessary, final compromise.

G en. [William] Heath. Mr. President, after a long and painful investigation of the federal Constitution by paragraphs, this honorable Convention is drawing nigh to the ultimate question—a question as momentous as ever invited the attention of man. We are soon to decide on a system of government, digested, not for the people of the commonwealth of Massachusetts only—not for the present people of the United States only—but, in addition to these, for all those states which may hereafter rise into existence within the jurisdiction of the United States, and for millions of people yet unborn; a system of government, not for a nation of slaves, but for a people as free and virtuous as any on earth; not for a conquered nation, subdued to our will, but for a people who have fought, who have bled, and who have conquered; who, under the smiles of Heaven, have established their independence and sovereignty, and have taken equal rank among the nations of the earth. In short, sir, it is a system of government for ourselves and for our children, for all that is near and dear to us in life; and on the decision of the question is suspended our political prosperity or infelicity, perhaps our existence as a nation. What can be more solemn? What can be more interesting? Everything depends on our union. I know that some have supposed, that, although the union should be broken, particular states may retain their importance, but this cannot be. The strongest-nerved state, even the right arm, if separated from the body, must wither. If the great union be broken our country, as a nation, perishes; and if our country so perishes, it will be as impossible to save a particular state as to preserve one of the fingers of a mortified hand.

A Majority Favor a Federal System

By one of the paragraphs of the system, it is declared that the ratifications of the conventions of nine states shall be sufficient for the establishment of the Constitution between the states so ratifying the same. But, sir, how happy will it be, if not only nine, but even all the states, should ratify it! It will be a happy circumstance if only a small majority of this Convention should ratify the federal system, but how much more happy if we could be unanimous! It will be a happy circumstance if a majority of the people of this common wealth should be in favor of the federal system; but how much more so, if they should be unanimous! And, if there are any means whereby they may be united, every exertion should be made to effect it. I presume, sir, that there is not a single gentleman within these walls who does not wish for a federal government—for an efficient federal government; and that this government should be possessed of every power necessary to enable it to shed on the people the benign influence of a good government. But I have observed, from the first, that many gentlemen appear opposed to the system; and this, I apprehend, arises from their objections to some particular parts of it. Is there not a way in which their minds may be relieved from embarrassment? I think there is; and if there is, no exertions should be spared in endeavoring to do it.

If we should ratify the Constitution, and instruct our first members to Congress to exert their endeavors to have such checks and guards provided as appear to be necessary in some of the paragraphs of the Constitution, communicate what we may judge proper to our sister states, and request their concurrence, is there not the highest probability that every thing which we wish may be effectually secured? I think there is, and I cannot but flatter myself that in this way the gentlemen of the Convention will have the difficulties under which they now labor removed from their minds. We shall be united; the people of this commonwealth and our sister states may be united. Permit me, therefore, most earnestly to recommend it to the serious consideration of every gentleman in this honorable Convention. . . .

Proposal of Amendments

[John Hancock] When the Convention met in the afternoon,

his excellency, the President observed that a motion had been made and seconded, that this Convention do assent to and ratify the Constitution which had been under consideration; and that he had, in the former part of the day, intimated his intention of submitting a proposition to the Convention. My motive, says he, arises from my earnest desire to this Convention, my fellow-citizens and the public at large, that this Convention may adopt such a form of government as may extend its good influence to every part of the United States and advance the prosperity of the whole world. His situation, his excellency said, had not permitted him to enter into the debates of this Convention. It, however, appeared to him necessary, from what had been advanced in them, to adopt the form of government proposed; but, observing a diversity of sentiment in the gentlemen of the Convention, he had frequently had conversation with them on the subject, and from this conversation with them on the subject, and from this conversation he was induced to propose to them, whether the introduction of some general amendments would not be attended with the happiest consequences. . . .

Hon. Mr. [Samuel] Adams. . . . I have said that I have had my doubts of this Constitution. I could not digest every part of it as readily as some gentlemen; but his, sir, is my misfortune, not my fault. Other gentlemen have had their doubts; but, in my opinion, the proposition submitted will have a tendency to remove such doubts, and to conciliate the minds of the Convention, and the people without doors. This subject, sir, is of the greatest magnitude and has employed the attention of every rational man in the United States, but the minds of the people are not so well agreed on it as all of us could wish. A proposal of this sort, coming from Massachusetts, from her importance, will have it weight. Four or five states have considered and ratified the Constitution as it stands; but we know there is a diversity of opinion even in these states, and one of them is greatly agitated. If this Convention should particularize the amendments necessary to be proposed, it appears to me it must have weight in other states, where Conventions have not yet met. I have observed the sentiments of gentlemen on the subject as far as Virginia, and I have found that the objections were similar in the newspapers and in some of the Conventions. Considering these circumstances, it appears to me that such a measure will have the most salutary effect throughout the Union. It is of the greatest importance that *America* should still be united in sentiment. I think I have not, heretofore, been unmindful of the advantage of such a union. It is essential that the people should be united in the federal government, to withstand the common enemy and to preserve their valuable rights and liberties. We find, in the great state of Pennsylvania, one third of the Convention are opposed to it; should, then, there be large minorities in the several states, I should fear the consequences of such disunion. . . .

The only difficulty on gentlemen's minds is, whether it is best to accept this Constitution on conditional amendments, or to rely on amendments in future, as the Constitution

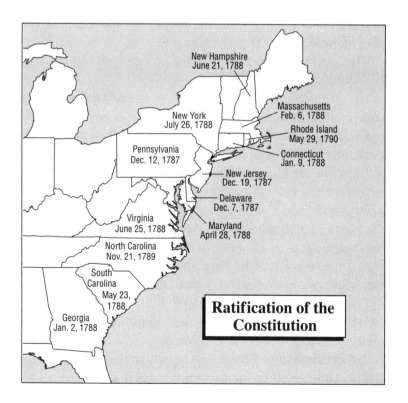

New Hampshire
June 21, 1788

New York
July 26, 1788

Massachusetts
Feb. 6, 1788

Rhode Island
May 29, 1790

Connecticut
Jan. 9, 1788

Pennsylvania
Dec. 12, 1787

New Jersey
Dec. 19, 1787

Delaware
Dec. 7, 1787

Virginia
June 25, 1788

Maryland
April 28, 1788

North Carolina
Nov. 21, 1789

South
Carolina
May 23,
1788

Georgia
Jan. 2, 1788

Ratification of the Constitution

provides. When I look over the article which provides for a revision, I have my doubts. Suppose, sir, nine states accept the Constitution without any conditions at all, and the four states should wish to have amendments. Where will you find nine states to propose, and the legislatures of nine states to agree to, the introduction of amendments? Therefore, it seems to me that the expectation of amendments taking place at some future time will be frustrated. This method, if we take it, will be the most likely to bring about the amendments, as the Conventions of New Hampshire, Rhode Island, New York, Maryland, Virginia and South Carolina, have not yet met. I apprehend, sir, that these states will be influenced by the proposition which your excellency has submitted, as the resolutions of Massachusetts have ever had their influence. If this should be the case, the necessary amendments would be introduced more early and more safely. From these considerations, as your excellency did not think it proper to make a motion, with submission, I move that the paper read by your excellency be now taken under consideration by the Convention.

The motion being seconded, the proposition was read by the secretary at the table.

Dr. [John] Taylor liked the idea of amendments; but, he said, he did not see any constitutional door open for the introduction of them by the Convention. He read the several authorities which provided for the meeting of Conventions, but did not see in any of them any power given to propose amendments. We are, he said, therefore, treading on unsafe ground to propose them; we must take the whole or reject the whole. The honorable gentleman was in favor of the adjournment, and, in a speech of some length, deprecated the consequences, which, he said, must arise, if the Constitution was adopted or rejected by a small majority. . . .

[Wednesday, Feb. 6, 1788] REV. [Samuel] Stillman. Mr. President, I rise, with deference to gentlemen of superior abilities, to give my opinion on the present all-important national question, and the reasons on which it is founded—an opinion, the result of the most serious deliberation.

Upon entering the Convention, it was my full determination to keep my mind cool and open to conviction, that so I might profit by the discussion of this interesting subject; and now, sir, return my sincere thanks to the gentlemen who have taken opposite sides in the course of the debates. From both I have received advantage—from one class in bringing forward a great variety of objections; from the other class in answering them. Whatever my previous opinion was, I now stand on firmer ground than ever respecting the proposed Constitution. . . .

I have no interest to influence me to accept this Constitution of government, distinct from the interest of my countrymen at large. We are all embarked in one bottom and must sink or swim together.

Besides, sir, Heaven has fixed me in a line a duty that precludes every prospect of the honors and the emoluments [benefits] of office. Let who will govern, I must obey. Nor would I exchange the pulpit for the highest honors my country can confer. I, too, have personal liberties to secure, as dear to me as to any gentlemen in the Convention, and as numerous a family, probably, to engage my attention; besides which, I stand here, with my very honorable colleagues, as a representative of the citizens of this great metropolis, who have been pleased to honor me with their confidence—an honor, in my view, unspeakably greater than a peerage or a pension.

The absolute deficiency of the Articles of Confederation is allowed by all. Nor have I seen any publication that places this subject in so convincing a point of view as a letter written by his excellency, [Virginia] Governor [Edmund] Randolph, which has appeared in several of our newspapers; whom I the rather introduce, on this occasion because he was a delegate in the late federal Convention, refused to sign the Constitution before us and has been twice mentioned by gentlemen in the opposition. His candor, apparent in the letter referred to, does him honor, and merits the esteem of every candid mind. I declare, sir, I revere his character, while I differ from him in opinion.

"Before my departure for the (federal) Convention," says he, "I believed that the Confederation was not so eminently defective as it had been supposed. But after I had entered into a free conversation with those who were best informed of the condition and interest of each state—after I had compared the intelligence derived from them with the properties that ought to characterize the government of our Union—I became persuaded that the Confederation was destitute of *every energy* which a constitution of the United States ought to possess." And after he had, in the most masterly manner, proved its insufficiency, he adds, "But now, sir, permit me to declare that, in my humble judgment, the powers by which alone the blessings of a general government can be accomplished, cannot be interwoven in the Confederation, *without a change of its very essence;* or, in other words, that the Confederation *must be thrown aside.*" Having stated his objections to it, he proceeds thus: "My inference from these facts and principles is that the new powers must be deposited in a new body, growing out of the consolidation of the Union, as far as the circumstance of the states would allow." Thus fully and candidly does this gentleman insist on the absolute necessity of a new constitution of general government, at the very time that he objected to the present form; and [he] concludes his letter with these memorable words, which I most heartily wish may make a deep impression on the mind of every gentleman in the opposition: "I hesitate not to say, that the most fervent prayer of my soul is, the establishment of a firm, energetic government; that the most inveterate curse that can befall us is a dissolution of the Union and that the *present moment,* if suffered to pass unemployed, can NEVER be recalled. I shall therefore cling to the Union as the rock of our salvation, and urge Virginia to finish the salutary work which she hath begun. And if, after our best efforts for amendments, they cannot be obtained, I scruple not to declare (notwithstanding the advantage the declaration may give to the enemies of my proposal) that I will, as an individual citizen, accept the Constitution."

I pause, sir, that every gentleman present may have time to indulge those feelings which these excellent expressions must occasion. May that God, who has the hearts of all men under his control, inspire every member of this Convention with a similar disposition! Then shall we lay aside every opposite interest and unite, as a band of brothers in the ratification of this Constitution of national government.

Ratify With or Without Amendments

Then, sir, will your terms of conciliation be attended to with gratitude and candor. Your excellency, depressed with bodily infirmity, and excercised with severe pain, has stepped forth at the critical moment, and, from the benevolence of your heart, presented us with a number of proposed amendments, in order, if possible, to quiet the minds of the gentlemen in the opposition and bring us together in amity and peace—amendments which you, sir, declare you do not think necessary, except for the sole purpose of uniting us in a common and most important cause.

But what has been the consequence of your excellency's conciliatory propositions? Jealousy—jealousy, sir, that there was a snake in the grass, a secret intention to deceive. I shuddered at the ungenerous suggestion, nor will I dwell a moment longer on the distressing idea. Be banished forever the groundless suspicion of him whose name stands foremost in the list of American patriots! Let love and harmony prevail!

The important hour is just arrived when the die will be cast, that will in a great measure determine the fate of this commonwealth and have a mighty influence on the general interests of the Union; for, from the best information I have been able to collect from gentlemen of observation and of undoubted veracity, there is the greatest reason to fear that the rejection of this Constitution will be followed with anarchy and confusion. . . .

Viewing the Constitution in this light, I stand ready to give my vote for it, without any amendments at all. Yet, if the amendments proposed by your excellency will tend to conciliation, I readily admit them, not as a condition of acceptance, but as a matter of recommendation only; knowing that blessed are the peace-makers. I am ready, sir, to submit my life, my liberty, my family, my property, and, as far as my vote will go, the interest of my constituents, to this general government. . . .

Amendments Are a Moral Certainty

Hon. [Capt. John] Turner. Mr. President, being advanced in life and having endeavored, I hope, with a faithful attention, according to my ability, to assist my country in their trying difficulties and dangers for more than twenty years; and as, for three weeks past, my state of health has been such as to render me unable to speak in this assembly, I trust I shall be heard with some indulgence, while I express a few senti-

The Battle for Ratification

Winton U. Solberg, an eminent historian from Yale and currently professor emeritus at the University of Illinois, explains that achieving the nine states necessary to implement the Constitution started out strongly, but, as the goal approached, the states began to become more reticent. Many later states would only agree to ratify the Constitution if amendments were made to it. Federalists agreed to these amendments rather than risk a second convention.

T he ratification struggle began with Federalists and Antifederalists marshaling forces as soon as Congress submitted the Constitution to the states. The latter possessed able leaders and arguments which met widespread support. Most important of these were fear of the taxing power, lack of a bill of rights, and the scale of representation. In vain did Federalists iterate a position implied in Convention debates—that no bill of rights was needed, since all powers not delegated to Congress were reserved—to the people or the states. Antifederalists gained by insisting on explicit guarantees demanded by those who believed popular rights could not be over protected. Likewise, anxiety over national collapse arising from the notion that republicanism could not

ments at this solemn crisis. I have been averse to the reception of this Constitution, while it was considered merely in its original form, but, since the honorable Convention have pleased to agree to the recommendation of certain amendments, I acknowledge my mind is reconciled. But even thus amended, I still see, or think I see, several imperfections in it, and some which give me pain. Indeed, I never expect to see a constitution free from imperfections; and, considering the great diversity of local interests, views and habits—considering the unparalleled variety of sentiments among the citizens of the United States—I despair of obtaining a more perfect constitution than this, at present. And a constitution preferable to the Confederation must be obtained, and obtained soon, or we shall be an undone people.

---

endure in a large territory led to insistence that government be brought closer to the governed. This meant reducing the scale of representation and increasing the number of representatives.

Despite several spirited contests the requisite number of states adopted the Constitution within nine months after submission to them. The first five accepted in short statements, often of one paragraph, which imposed no qualification. To achieve this in Pennsylvania necessitated force to obtain a quorum and buying up of opposition newspapers. However, Federalists preferred to accept amendments rather than risk ruin or a second convention, and in ratifying and at the same time recommending improvements Massachusetts discovered a formula which was used in all subsequent cases except Maryland.

Since there could be no hope of firm union without Virginia and New York, attention focused on the close struggles pending in these states when New Hampshire, the ninth state, completed the bond. After prolonged debate the Virginia Convention facilitated adoption of the Constitution by using the Massachusetts technique.

Winton U. Solberg, *The Federal Convention and the Formation of the Union of the American States.* New York: Liberal Arts Press, 1958, p. 306.

In my judgment, there is a rational probability, a moral certainty, that the proposed amendments will meet the approbation of the several states in the Union. If there is any respect due to the hoary head of Massachusetts, it will undoubtedly have its proper influence in this case. The minds of gentlemen throughout the nation must be impressed with such a sense of the necessity of all-important union, especially in our present circumstances, as must strongly operate in favor of a concurrence. The proposed amendments are of such a liberal, such a generous, and such a catholic nature and complexion—they are so congenial to the soul of every man who is possessed of patriotic regard to the preservation of the just rights and immunities of his country, as well as to the institution of a good and necessary government—that I think they must, they will, be universally accepted. . . . I find myself constrained to say, before this assembly, and before God, that I think it my duty to give my vote in favor of this Constitution with the proposed amendments; and, unless some further light shall be thrown in my way to influence my opinion, I shall conduct accordingly. I know not whether this Convention will vote a ratification of this Constitution or not. If they should do it and have the concurrence of the other states, may that God, who has always, in a remarkable manner watched over us and our fathers for good, in all difficulties, dangers, and distresses, be pleased to command his almighty blessing upon it, and make it instrumental of restoring justice, honor, safety, support and salvation, to a sinking land! . . . I believe your excellency's patience will not be further exercised by hearing the sound of my voice on the occasion, when I have said, May the United States of America live before God! May they be enlightened, pious, virtuous, free, and happy, to all generations! . . .

John Hancock, the President, rose, and addressed the honorable Convention as follows:

Gentlemen, being now called upon to bring the subject under debate to a decision, by bringing forward the question, I beg your indulgence to close the business with a few words. I am happy that my health has been so far restored that I am rendered able to meet my fellow-citizens as represented in this Convention. I should have considered it as one of the most distressing misfortunes of my life to be deprived of giving my aid and support to a system, which, if amended (as I feel assured it will be) according to your proposals, cannot fail to give the people of the United States a greater degree of political freedom, and eventually as much national dignity as falls to the lot of any nation on earth. I have not, since I had the honor to be in this place, said much on the important subject before us. All the ideas appertaining to the system, as well those which are against as for it, have been debated upon with so much learning and ability that the subject is quite exhausted.

But you will permit me, gentlemen, to close the whole with one or two general observations. This I request, not expecting to throw any new light on the subject but because it may possibly prevent uneasiness and discordance from taking place amongst us and amongst our constituents.

That a general system of government is indispensably necessary to save our country from ruin is agreed upon all sides. That the one now to be decided upon has its defects, all agree; but when we consider the variety of interests, and the different habits of the men it is intended for, it would be very singular to have an entire union of sentiment respecting it. Were the people of the United States to delegate the powers proposed to be given to men who were not dependent on them frequently for elections—to men whose interest, either from rank or title, would differ from that of their fellow-citizens in common—the task of delegating authority would be vastly more difficult; but, as the matter now stands, the powers reserved by the people render them secure, and, until they themselves become corrupt, they will always have upright and able rulers. I give my assent to the Constitution, in full confidence that the amendments proposed will soon become a part of the system. These amendments being in no wise local, but, calculated to give security and ease alike to all the states, I think that all will agree to them.

Suffer me to add, that, let the question be decided as it may, there can be no triumph on the one side or chagrin on the other. Should there be a great division, every good man, every man who loves this country, will be so far from exhibiting extraordinary marks of joy that he will sincerely lament the want of unanimity and strenuously endeavor to cultivate a spirit of conciliation, both in Convention and at home. The people of this commonwealth are a people of great light—of great intelligence in public business. They know that we have none of us an interest separate from theirs, that it must be our happiness to conduce to theirs and that we must all rise or fall together. They will never, therefore, forsake the first principle of society—that of being governed by the voice of the majority. And should it be that the proposed form of government should be rejected, they will zealously attempt another. Should it, by the vote now to be taken, be ratified, they will quietly acquiesce, and where they see a want of perfection in it, endeavor, in a constitutional way, to have it amended.

The question now before you is such as no nation on earth, without the limits of America, has ever had the privilege of deciding upon. As the Supreme Ruler of the universe has seen fit to bestow upon us this glorious opportunity, let us decide upon it; appealing to him for the rectitude of our intentions, and in humble confidence that he will yet continue to bless and save our country.

The Resolve of the Committee

The question being put, whether this Convention will accept of the report of the committee, as follows: . . .

The Convention, having impartially discussed and fully considered the Constitution for the United States of America, reported to Congress by the Convention of delegates a resolution of the General Court of the said commonwealth, passed the twenty-fifth day of October last past; and acknowledging, with grateful hearts, the goodness of the Supreme Ruler of the universe in affording the people of the United States, in the course of his providence, an opportunity, deliberately and peaceably, without fraud or surpirse, of entering into an explicit and solemn compact with each other, by assenting to and ratifying a new Constitution, in order to form a more perfect union, establish justice, insure domestic tranquillity, provide for the common defence, promote the general welfare, and secure the blessings of liberty to themselves and their posterity, DOES, in the name and in behalf of the people of the commonwealth of Massachusetts, assent to and ratify the said Constitution for the United States of America.

And, as it is the opinion of this Convention, that certain amendments and alterations in the said Constitution would remove the fears and quiet the apprehensions of many of the good people of the commonwealth and more effectually guard against an undue administration of the federal government, the Convention DOES therefore recommend that . . . alterations and provisions be introduced into the said Constitution. . . . And the Convention DOES, in the name and in the behalf of the people of this commonwealth, enjoin it upon their representatives in Congress, at all times, until the alterations and provisions . . . have been considered, agreeably to the 5th article of the said Constitution, to exert all their influence, and use all reasonable and legal methods, to obtain a ratification of the . . . alterations and provisions, in such manner as is provided in the said article.

And, that the United States, in Congress assembled, may have due notice of the assent and ratification of the said Constitution by this Convention.

Ambivalence Toward a Bill of Rights

James Madison

> The first ten amendments to the U.S. Constitution are collectively known as the Bill of Rights. Many people consider them one of the primary strengths of the U.S. Constitution. But, originally, the Constitution had no such Bill of Rights. In fact, James Madison, a primary contributor to the U.S. Constitution, often expressed the belief that a Bill of Rights was not necessary in a government that is properly constructed. In this letter to Thomas Jefferson, written on October 17, 1788, after many states had ratified the Constitution only with the understanding that a Bill of Rights must be added to the document, Madison reluctantly accepts the idea that a Bill of Rights should be part of the U.S. Constitution. As he is expressing his support for a Bill of Rights, Madison continues to question the wisdom of adding them to the Constitution, leaving the impression that his support for a Bill of Rights is more a matter of political expedience, not a fundamental change of heart.

My own opinion has always been in favor of a bill of rights, provided it be so framed as not to imply powers not meant to be included in the enumeration. At the same time, I have never thought the omission a material defect, nor been anxious to supply it even by *subsequent* amendment, for any other reason than that it is anxiously desired by others. I have favored it because I supposed it might be

From James Madison's October 17, 1788, letter to Thomas Jefferson, as reprinted in *The Papers of James Madison,* vol. 11, *7 March 1788–1 March 1789,* edited by Robert A. Rutland and Charles F. Hobson (Charlottesville: University Press of Virginia, 1977).

of use and, if properly executed, could not be of disservice. I have not viewed it in an important light: 1. because I conceive that in a certain degree, though not in the extent argued by Mr. [James] Wilson, the rights in question are reserved by the manner in which the federal powers are granted. 2 because there is great reason to fear that a positive declaration of some of the most essential rights could not be obtained in the requisite latitude. I am sure that the rights of Conscience in particular, if submitted to public definition would be narrowed much more than they are likely ever to be by an assumed power. One of the objections in New England was that the Constitution by prohibiting religious tests opened a door for Jews Turks & infidels. 3. because the limited powers of the federal Government and the jealousy of the subordinate governments afford a security which has not existed in the case of the state governments and exists in no other. 4 because experience proves the inefficacy of a bill of rights on those occasions when its control is most needed. Repeated violations of these parchment barriers have been committed by overbearing majorities in every state. In Virginia I have seen the bill of rights violated in every instance where it has been opposed to a popular current. Notwithstanding the explicit provision contained in that instrument for the rights of conscience it is well known that a religious establishment would have taken place in that state, if the legislative majority had found as they expected, a majority of the people in favor of the measure; and I am persuaded that if a majority of the people were now of one sect, the measure would still take place and on narrower ground than was then proposed, notwithstanding the additional obstacle which the law has since created.

No Safeguard Against Abuse of Power

Wherever the real power in a government lies, there is the danger of oppression. In our governments the real power lies in the majority of the community, and the invasion of private rights is *cheifly* to be apprehended, not from acts of government contrary to the sense of its constituents, but from acts in which the government is the mere instrument of the major number of the constituents. This is a truth of great importance, but not yet sufficiently attended to. [It] is probably more strongly impressed on my mind by facts, and reflections suggested by them, than on yours which has contemplated abuses of power issuing from a very different quarter. Wherever there is an interest and power to do wrong, wrong will generally be done, and not less readily by a powerful & interested party than by a powerful and interested prince. The difference, so far as it relates to the superiority of republics over monarchies, lies in the less degree of probability that interest may prompt abuses of power in the former than in the latter; and in the security in the former against oppression of more than the smaller part of the society, whereas in the former it may be extended in a manner to the whole. The difference so far as it relates to the point in question—the efficacy of a bill of rights in controuling abuses of power—lies in this, that in a monarchy the latent force of the nation is superior to that of the sovereign, and a solemn charter of popular rights must have a great effect, as a standard for trying the validity of public acts, and a signal for rousing and uniting the superior force of the community; whereas in a popular government, the political and physical power may be considered as vested in the same hands, that is in a majority of the people, and consequently the tyrannical will of the sovereign is not to be controled by the dread of an appeal to any other force within the community. What use then it may be asked can a bill of rights serve in popular governments? I answer the two following which though less essential than in other governments, sufficiently recommend the precaution: 1. The political truths declared in that solemn manner acquire by degrees the character of fundamental maxims of free government, and as they become incorporated with the national sentiment, counteract the impulses of interest and passion. 2. Although it be generally true as above stated that the danger of oppression lies in the interested majorities of the people rather than in usurped acts of the government, yet there may be occasions on which the evil may spring from the latter sources; and on such, a bill of rights will be a good ground for an appeal to the sense of the community. Perhaps, too, there may be a certain degree of danger that a succession of artful and ambitious rulers may, by gradual & well–timed advances, finally erect an independent government on the subversion of liberty. Should this danger exist at all, it is prudent to guard against it, especially when the precaution can do no injury. At the same time I must own that I see no tendency in our governments to danger on that side. It has been remarked that there is a tendency in all governments to an augmentation of power at the expence of liberty. But the remark as usually understood does not appear to me well founded. Power when it has attained a certain degree of energy and independence goes on generally to further degrees. But when below that degree, the direct tendency is to further degrees of relaxation, until the abuses of liberty beget a sudden transition to an undue degree of power. With this explanation the remark may be true, and in the latter sense only is it in my opinion applicable to the governments in America. It is a melancholy reflection that liberty should be equally exposed to danger whether the government have too much or too little power, and that the line which divides these extremes should be so inaccurately defined by experience.

The Bill Can Have No Power Against a Majority Will

Supposing a bill of rights to be proper, the articles which ought to compose it admit of much discussion. I am inclined to think that *absolute* restrictions in cases that are doubtful, or where emergencies may overrule them, ought to be avoided. The restrictions however strongly marked on paper will never be regarded when opposed to the decided sense of the public; and after repeated violations in extraordinary cases, they will lose even their ordinary efficacy. Should a rebellion or insurrection alarm the people as well as the government, and a suspension of the habeas corpus be dictated by the alarm, no written prohibitions on earth would prevent the measure. Should an army in time of peace be gradually established in our neighborhood by Britain or Spain, declarations on paper would have as little effect in preventing a standing force for the public safety. The best security against these evils is to remove the pretext for them. With regard to monopolies they are justly classed among the greatest nusances in government. But is it clear that, as encouragements to literary works and ingenious discoveries, they are not too valuable to be wholly renounced? Would it not suffice to reserve in all cases a right to the public to abolish the privilege at a price to be specified in the grant of it? Is there not also infinitely less danger of this abuse in our governments than in most others? Monopolies are sacrifices of the many to the few. Where the power is in the few, it is natural for them to sacrifice the many to their own partialities and corruptions. Where the power, as with us, is in the many not in the few, the danger can not be very great that the few will be thus favored. It is much more to be dreaded that the few will be unnecessarily sacrificed to the many.

The Need for
a Bill of Rights

Thomas Jefferson

Not surprisingly for the author of the Declaration of Independence—with its emphasis on the rights of life, liberty, and pursuit of happiness—Thomas Jefferson wished to see a government that protected individual liberties from government interference. Therefore, he strongly believed that a Bill of Rights could only strengthen the U.S. Constitution. To those critics who argue that no Bill of Rights could list all freedoms that must be protected and thus the attempt should never be made, Jefferson's reply is clear: "half a loaf is better than no bread." In this letter dated March 15, 1789, to James Madison, one such critic against a Bill of Rights (and primary architect of the Constitution), Jefferson endeavors to convince Madison that a Bill of Rights strengthens American democracy. Knowing that he had won the argument, in the sense that a Bill of Rights would be added to the U.S. Constitution, Jefferson gently suggests that the addition of a Bill of Rights is not simply a political necessity to get the states to ratify the Constitution.

Your thoughts on the subject of the Declaration of rights in the letter of Oct. 17. I have weighed with great satisfaction. Some of them had not occurred to me before but were acknowledged just in the moment they were presented to my mind. In the arguments in favor of a declaration of

From Thomas Jefferson's March 15, 1789, letter to James Madison, as reprinted in *The Papers of Thomas Jefferson,* vol. 14, *8 October 1788–26 March 1789,* edited by Julian P. Boyd (Princeton, NJ: Princeton University Press, 1958).

rights, you omit one which has great weight with me, the legal check which it puts into the hands of the judiciary. This is a body which, if rendered independent and kept strictly to their own department, merits great confidence for their learning and integrity. . . .

The Good Outweighs the Evil

I am happy to find that on the whole you are a friend to this amendment. The declaration of rights is like all other human blessings—alloyed with some inconveniences and not accomplishing fully its object. But the good in this instance vastly overweighs the evil. I cannot refrain from making short answers to the objections which your letter states to have been raised. 1. That the rights in questions are reserved by the manner in which the federal powers are granted. Answer: A constitutive act may certainly be so formed as to need no declaration of rights. The act itself has the force of a declaration as far as it goes. If it goes to all material points, nothing more is wanting. In the draft of a constitution which I had once a thought of proposing in Virginia and printed afterwards, I endeavored to reach all the great objects of public liberty and did mean to add a declaration of rights. Probably the object was imperfectly executed, but the deficiencies would have been supplied by others in the course of discussion. But in a constitutive act which leaves some precious articles unnoticed, and raises implications against others, a declaration of rights becomes necessary by way of supplement. This is the case of our new federal constitution. This instrument forms us into one state as to certain objects and gives us a legislative and executive body for these objects. It should therefore guard us against their abuses of power within the field submitted to them. 2. A positive declaration of some essential rights could not be obtained in the requisite latitude. Answer: Half a loaf is better than no bread. If we cannot secure all our rights, let us secure what we can. 3. The limited powers of the federal government and jealousy of the subordinate governments afford a security which exists in no other instance. Answer: The first member of this seems resolvable into the first objection before stated. The jealousy of the subordinate governments are only agents. They must have principles furnished them whereon to found their opposition. The declaration of rights will be the text whereby they will try all the acts of the federal government. In this view it is necessary to the federal government also: as by the same text they may try the opposition of the subordinate governments. 4. Experience proves the inefficacy of a bill of rights. True. But though it is not absolutely efficacious under all circumstances, it is of great potency always, and rarely inefficacious. A brace the more will often keep up the building which would have fallen with the brace the less. There is a remarkeable difference between the characters of the inconveniencies which attend a declaration of rights, and those which attend the want of it. The inconveniences of the declaration are that it may cramp government in its useful exertions. But the evil of this is short-lived, moderate and reparable. The inconveniencies of the want of a declaration are permanent, afflicting and irreparable; they are in constant progression from bad to worse.

A Safeguard Against Any Form of Tyranny

The executive in our governments is not the sole—it is scarcely the principal—object of my jealousy. The tyranny of the legislatures is the most formidable dread at present and will be for long years. That of the executive will come in its turn, but it will be at a remote period. I know there are some among us who would now establish a monarchy. But they are inconsiderable in number and weight of character. The rising race are all republicans. We were educated in royalism: no wonder if some of us retain that idolatry still. Our young people are educated in republicanism. An apostasy [a surrender of faith] from that to royalism is unprecedented and impossible. I am much pleased with the prospect that a declaration of rights will be added and hope it will be done in that way which will not endanger the whole frame of the government, or any essential part of it.

Appendix: The Delegates to the Constitutional Convention

*Signer of the U.S. Constitution

Connecticut
Oliver Ellsworth
William Samuel
    Johnson*
Roger Sherman*

Delaware
Richard Bassett*
Gunning Bedford Jr.*
Jacob Broom*
John Dickinson*
George Read*

Georgia
Abraham Baldwin*
William Few*
William Houstoun
William Pierce

Maryland
Daniel Carroll*
Daniel of St. Thomas
    Jenifer*
Luther Martin

James McHenry*
John Francis Mercer

Massachusetts
Elbridge Gerry
Nathaniel Gorham*
Rufus King*
Caleb Strong

New Hampshire
Nicholas Gilman*
John Langdon*

New Jersey
David Brearly*
Jonathan Dayton*
William Churchill Houston
William Livingston*
William Paterson*

New York
Alexander Hamilton*
John Lansing Jr.
Robert Yates

North Carolina

William Blount*
William Richardson Davie
Alexander Martin
Richard Dobbs Spaight*
Hugh Williamson*

Pennsylvania

George Clymer*
Thomas Fitzsimons*
Benjamin Franklin*
Jared Ingersoll*
Thomas Mifflin*
Gouverneur Morris*
Robert Morris*
James Wilson*

South Carolina

Pierce Butler*
Charles Pinckney*
Charles Cotesworth
  Pinckney*
John Rutledge*

Virginia

John Blair*
James Madison Jr.*
George Mason
James McClurg
Edmund Randolph
George Washington*
George Wythe

Chronology

1776
The Continental Congress signs and adopts the Declaration of Independence on July 4.

1777
The Continental Congress adopts the Articles of Confederation and sends them to the states for their ratification.

1781
On January 2 Virginia relinquishes its claims on its western lands (now the state of Kentucky) convincing Maryland, the only holdout, to ratify the Articles of Confederation; the Articles of Confederation become the first system of government of the United States of America.

1786
On August 15 Shays's Rebellion begins; the Annapolis Convention, attended only by five states, takes place from September 11–14 and issues a resolution calling for another convention to be held in May 1787 to discuss ways of strengthening the Articles of Confederation.

1787
February 4: The Massachusetts militia defeats Daniel Shays and his followers at Petersham, Massachusetts; this is the last formal military engagement of Shays's Rebellion.

February 21: Congress adopts the Annapolis resolution, calling for a convention to be held in Philadelphia in May 1787.

May 14: The Constitutional Convention is scheduled to begin in Philadelphia; however, not enough states have arrived to achieve a quorum of seven states.

May 25: The first day of the Convention; George Washington is unanimously elected president of the convention.

May 29: Edmund Randolph presents the Virginia Plan, calling for a two-chamber legislature, where representation in both houses would be based on state population.

June 15: William Paterson presents the New Jersey Plan, calling for a one-chamber legislature in which each state would have the same number of representatives.

June 19: The convention rejects the New Jersey Plan.

July 16: The convention accepts the Great Compromise; the Great Compromise proposes a two-chamber legislature, with one house (the House of Representatives) based on population and the other house (the Senate) with equal representation for all states.

July 26–August 5: The convention goes into recess.

July 26: The Committee of Detail prepares the first draft of the Constitution.

August 6: The convention reconvenes; the convention continues to debate various aspects of the Constitution, including the election method of the president and how slaves will be counted for population purposes.

September 6: The convention appoints the Committee on Style and Arrangement to prepare a revised draft of the Constitution.

September 12: The convention rejects a proposal to include a bill of rights in the Constitution.

September 17: Benjamin Franklin urges all delegates to sign the Constitution; Edmund Randolph, George Mason, and Elbridge Gerry refuse to sign the Constitution; thirty-nine delegates, representing all twelve states that have sent delegates, sign the U.S. Constitution; the convention dissolves.

September 19: The *Pennsylvania Packet* is the first newspaper to publish the Constitution.

September 20: The Confederation Congress receives the Constitution.

September 28: Congress submits the Constitution to the states for their consideration and ratification.

December 7: Delaware ratifies the Constitution unanimously and become the first state to ratify the U.S. Constitution.

December 12: Pennsylvania ratifies the Constitution, 46 votes to 23.

December 18: New Jersey ratifies the Constitution unanimously.

1788
January 2: Georgia ratifies the Constitution unanimously.

January 9: Connecticut ratifies the Constitution, 128 to 40.

February 6: Massachusetts ratifies the Constitution, 187 to 168; Massachusetts, in a strategy adopted by many subsequent states, adopts a list of recommended amendments to the Constitution to reflect its perceived weaknesses of the document.

March 24: Rhode Island town meetings reject the Constitution, 2,708 to 237; Rhode Island is the first state to reject the Constitution.

April 28: Maryland ratifies the Constitution, 63 to 11.

May 23: South Carolina ratifies the Constitution, 149 to 73, and adopts a list of recommended amendments.

June 21: New Hampshire ratifies the Constitution, 57 to 47, and adopts a list of recommended amendments.

June 25: Virginia ratifies the Constitution, 89 to 79, and adopts a list of recommended amendments.

July 2: The Confederation Congress announces New Hampshire's ratification of the Constitution; as the ninth state to ratify the Constitution, New Hampshire's vote effectively makes the Constitution the supreme law of the land.

July 26: New York ratifies the Constitution, 30 to 27, and adopts a list of recommended amendments.

August 2: North Carolina postpones a vote on ratification, and proposes a list of amendments to be adopted before the state convention will agree to ratify the Constitution.

1789
March 4: Effective date of the U.S. Constitution.

April 6: George Washington is unanimously declared the first president of the United States; John Adams is declared the first vice president.

June 8: James Madison introduces a bill of rights in the House of Representatives.

September 25: Congress proposes the Bill of Rights.

November 20: New Jersey is the first state to ratify the Bill of Rights.

1790
On May 29 Rhode Island ratifies the Constitution, 34 to 32, and adopts a list of recommended amendments.

1791
Vermont becomes the first new state to be admitted to the Union; the Bill of Rights has been ratified by three-fourths of the states and is added to the U.S. Constitution.

For Further Research

John K. Alexander, *The Selling of the Constitutional Convention: A History of News Coverage*. Madison, WI: Madison House, 1990.

American Political Science Association and American Historical Association, eds., *This Constitution: Our Enduring Legacy*. Washington, DC: Congressional Quarterly, 1986.

Charles A. Beard, *An Economic Interpretation of the Constitution of the United States*. 2nd ed. New York: Macmillan, 1941.

Walter Hartwell Bennett, ed., *Letters from the Federal Farmer to the Republican*. Tuscaloosa: University of Alabama Press, 1978.

Richard Bernstein with Kym Rice, *Are We to Be a Nation?* Cambridge, MA: Harvard University Press, 1987.

Catherine Drinker Bowen, *Miracle at Philadelphia: The Story of the Constitutional Convention, May to September 1787*. Boston: Little, Brown, 1966.

Julian P. Boyd, et al. ed., *The Papers of Thomas Jefferson*, 28 Volumes. Princeton, NJ: Princeton University Press, 1950–2000.

Christopher Collier and James Lincoln Collier, *Decision in Philadelphia: The Constitutional Convention of 1787*. New York: Random House, 1986.

The Debates in the Several State Conventions on the Adoption of the Federal Constitution, as Recommended by the General Convention at Philadelphia in 1787. Vol. 2. Philadelphia: J.B. Lippincott, 1941.

Max Farrand, *The Framing of the Constitution of the United States*. New Haven, CT: Yale University Press, 1913.

John C. Fitzpatrick, ed., *The Writings of George Washington from the Original Manuscript Sources, 1745–1799,* 39 Volumes. Westport, CT: Greenwood, 1970.

———, *The Writings of George Washington from the Original Manuscript Sources, December. Vol. 29. 1786–June 18, 1788. Westport, CT: Greenwood, 1970.*

Alexander Hamilton, James Madison, and John Jay, *The Federalist.* Ed. Benjamin Fletcher Wright. Cambridge, MA: Belknap Press of Harvard University Press, 1961.

Albert Bushnell Hart, ed., *American History Told by Contemporaries. Vol. 3. National Expansion, 1783–1845.* New York: Macmillan, 1910.

M.J. Heale, *The Making of American Politics, 1750–1850.* New York: Longman, 1977.

Robert W. Hoffert, *A Politics of Tensions: The Articles of Confederation and American Political Ideas.* Boulder: University of Colorado Press, 1992.

Gaillard Hunt and James Brown Scott, eds., *The Debates in the Federal Convention of 1787 Which Framed the Constitution of the United States of America, Reported by James Madison, Delegate from the State of Virginia.* Westport, CT: Greenwood, 1970.

Kenneth Janda, Jeffrey Berry, and Jerry Goldman, *The Challenge of Democracy: Government in America.* 4th ed. Boston: Houghton Mifflin, 1995.

Richard W. Leopold, Arthur S. Link, and Stanley Coben, eds., *Problems in American History.* 3rd ed. Vol. 1. *Through Reconstruction.* Englewood Cliffs, NJ: Prentice-Hall, 1966.

Leonard W. Levy and Kenneth L. Karst, eds., *Encyclopedia of the American Constitution.* 2nd ed. New York: Macmillan Reference USA, 2000.

Leonard W. Levy and Dennis J. Mahoney, eds., *The Framing and Ratification of the Constitution.* New York: Macmillan, 1987.

Wilson Carey McWilliams and Michael T. Gibbons, eds., *The Federalists, the Antifederalists, and the American Political Tradition.* New York: Greenwood, 1992.

Brodus Mitchell and Louise Pearson Mitchell, *A Biography of the Constitution of the United States: Its Origin, Formation, Adoption, Interpretation.* 2nd ed. New York: Oxford University Press, 1975.

William Pierce, "Notes of William Pierce on the Federal Convention of 1787," *American Historical Review,* vol. 3, January 1898.

Clinton Rossiter, *1787: The Grand Convention.* New York: Macmillan, 1966.

Ralph A. Rossum and Gary L. McDowell, eds., *The American Founding: Politics, Statesmanship, and the Constitution.* Port Washington, NY: Kennikat, 1981.

Robert A. Rutland, ed., *The Papers of George Mason, 1725–1792.* Vol 3. *1787–1792.* Chapel Hill: University of North Carolina Press, 1970.

Robert A. Rutland et al., eds., *The Papers of James Madison.* 7 Volumes. Charlottesville: University Press of Virginia, 1977–1991.

Robert A. Rutland et al., eds., *The Papers of James Madison.* 10 Volumes. 27 Chicago: University of Chicago Press, 1962–1977.

Winton U. Solberg, *The Federal Convention and the Formation of the Union of the American States.* New York: Liberal Arts, 1958.

Harold Syrett, ed., *The Papers of Alexander Hamilton.* Vol. 2. *1779–1781.* New York: Columbia University Press, 1961.

U.S. Department of State, *Documentary History of the Constitution of the United States of America, 1886–1870.* Washington, DC: Department of State, 1905.

Charles Warren, *The Making of the Constitution.* New York: Barnes and Noble, 1967.

Index